SECOND EDITION

TRIATHLON 101

JOHN MORA

Human Kinetics

Library of Congress Cataloging-in-Publication Data

Mora, John, 1964-
 Triathlon 101 / John Mora. -- 2nd ed.
  p. cm.
 Includes bibliographical references and index.
 ISBN-13: 978-0-7360-7944-0 (soft cover)
 ISBN-10: 0-7360-7944-0 (soft cover)
 1. Triathlon. 2. Triathlon--Training. I. Title. II. Title: Triathlon one hundred one. III. Title: Triathlon
one hundred and one.
 GV1060.73.M67 2009
 796.42'57--dc22

                              2008052942

ISBN-10: 0-7360-7944-0 (print)   ISBN-10: 0-7360-8529-7 (Adobe PDF)
ISBN-13: 978-0-7360-7944-0 (print)   ISBN-13: 978-0-7360-8529-8 (Adobe PDF)

Acquisitions Editor: Laurel Plotzke; **Developmental Editor:** Anne Hall; **Assistant Editors:** Cory
Weber and Carla Zych; **Copyeditor:** Tom Hanlon; **Proofreader:** Kathy Bennett; **Indexer:** Dan Connolly;
Permission Manager: Martha Gullo; **Graphic Designer:** Joe Buck; **Graphic Artist:** Kim McFarland;
Cover Designer: Keith Blomberg; **Photographer (cover):** Human Kinetics/Tom Roberts; **Photographer
(interior):** John Mora, unless otherwise noted; photos on v, 3, 25, 49, 79, 90, 93, 94, 111, 143, 173 © Human
Kinetics; **Photo Asset Manager:** Laura Fitch; **Visual Production Assistant:** Joyce Brumfield; **Photo Pro-
duction Manager:** Jason Allen; **Art Manager:** Kelly Hendren; **Associate Art Manager:** Alan L. Wilborn;
Illustrators: Ben Boyd (cartoons) and Tim Offenstein (line art 73, 84); **Printer:** United Graphics

Human Kinetics books are available at special discounts for bulk purchase. Special editions or book excerpts
can also be created to specification. For details, contact the Special Sales Manager at Human Kinetics.

Printed in the United States of America   10 9 8 7 6 5 4 3 2 1

Human Kinetics
Web site: www.HumanKinetics.com

United States: Human Kinetics
P.O. Box 5076
Champaign, IL 61825-5076
800-747-4457
e-mail: humank@hkusa.com

Canada: Human Kinetics
475 Devonshire Road Unit 100
Windsor, ON N8Y 2L5
800-465-7301 (in Canada only)
e-mail: info@hkcanada.com

Europe: Human Kinetics
107 Bradford Road
Stanningley
Leeds LS28 6AT, United Kingdom
+44 (0) 113 255 5665
e-mail: hk@hkeurope.com

Australia: Human Kinetics
57A Price Avenue
Lower Mitcham, South Australia 5062
08 8372 0999
e-mail: info@hkaustralia.com

New Zealand: Human Kinetics
Division of Sports Distributors NZ Ltd.
P.O. Box 300 226 Albany
North Shore City
Auckland
0064 9 448 1207
e-mail: info@humankinetics.co.nz

To Guillermo, who introduced me to marathoning.

To Jose, who introduced Guillermo and me to triathlon.

And to Team Three Amigos: Guillermo, Jose, and myself—
we had the best uniforms of any triathlon team.
And we had some of the best times of our lives becoming triathletes.

Contents

Part III Tri-ing Your Best 109

Foreword

Chances are that you're reading this book because you want to begin your adventure in triathlons. We call it an adventure because that's the way both of us have looked at the sport. We each came from athletic and active families, so triathlon has always been our greatest adventure. That doesn't mean that we haven't had our challenges, as do most beginners. We both started in the sport in 1985. My family was mad about rugby and rowing, while Laura's family would all go do fun runs together. So, since both our families got us hooked on fitness early on, we developed a passion for being active.

As fun as triathlon was for us in the beginning, we both realized quickly that you need to put in the time to train in order to be competitive. For both of us, covering the distance was the greatest challenge. As for me, I realized my run was not up to scratch after working hard on my swim and bike techniques for many years. That realization caused me to work on improving my runs for the last 12 years too. Laura has focused on strength and endurance, which are the keys to consistency.

But we both tackled our individual challenges and have grown up with the sport through the years. It has required an enormous amount of patience and perseverance—as well as plenty of trial and error—to overcome our obstacles. And although you might not apire to become a professional triathlete, we think having that same positive attitude in overcoming obstacles will give you your own kind of success on the race course. Whether it's overcoming your open-water worries or running a mile without stopping, those first steps take lots of patience and perseverance too.

It's also important to avoid feeling overwhelmed. If you've never done the sport before, you might feel intimidated and hard pressed to find enough time to train and work. It can be a challenge to find the balance and the energy you need to stick to a training routine. Just take it one step at a time and train within your limits. Triathlon is challenging, but it's also possible for most people, especially when you consider the many choices of sprint-distance races or even a triathlon relay to get you started.

Above all, just remember that triathlon is supposed to be fun. For both Laura and me, triathlon is like one big adventure that we're addicted to. Every race is a different course, kind of like when we were kids and the obstacle courses at school were always a fun challenge. It's this sense of adventure that gives us passion for the sport.

If you always look at the sport as an adventure—including the challenges you need to overcome to finish your first triathlon—you'll become as addicted and passionate about it as we are!

Greg and Laura Bennett

Preface

Want to "tri" a triathlon? Why not? It might be easier and more fun than you think!

Do you have friends who have done a triathlon and wonder what it takes to finish such an event? Or maybe you've already completed one or two but want to learn more about training plans, equipment, and other necessities to increase your triathlon IQ. Perhaps you're a runner, cyclist, or swimmer, and you want to expand your repertoire. No matter what your motivation, prepare yourself for a fun and exciting sport that will challenge you in ways you never imagined.

You've probably heard of the Ironman Triathlon and might have seen television coverage of die-hard triathletes willing to swim, bike, and run until the dead of night to finish. But the truth is that most short-course (sprint-distance) triathlons take little more than one hour to complete and less time to train for than a half-marathon running race.

More and more people—no matter their background or athletic talent—are interested in cross-training and competing in triathlons. And, since you're reading this book, it's likely that you are part of that growing group. But just like anything new, you've probably got a few questions rattling around in your soon-to-be tri-athlete noggin.

- Which race should I do?
- How much time will it take to train?
- Do I need a wetsuit?
- What kind of bicycle do I need?
- What's the best training schedule?
- What should I eat the morning of a race?
- What's the best way to learn to swim in open water?

In this revised, enhanced, and retooled second edition of *Triathlon 101*, you'll find the answers to all these questions and more. This book answers your important questions in an easy-to-understand, informative, and practical way.

You'll find the answers you need quickly, without a lot of technical mumbo-jumbo or complicated information. In fact, I've simplified things for you by focusing on the keys to a great triathlon debut—the necessary, practical basics for a successful, safe introduction to this exhilarating sport.

In the likely event that you'll be bitten by the triathlon bug and want to make this a fun part of your new healthy lifestyle, you will want to learn more about more complex sports science topics down the road. But first things first. Discover, integrate, and master the foundational information you find here, and use it as a stepping-stone to triathlon success.

No more searching around for the bits and pieces of the multisport puzzle from books that deal with a range of triathlon topics and skill levels. Forget about the hit-or-miss advice you might get from well-meaning friends or family. Finally, here is your one-stop resource that has all the information you need, in plain, simple language.

Triathlon 101 is divided into three parts. Part I covers all you need to know to plan your training and racing season, including information about equipment such as wetsuits and triathlon bikes. In chapters 1 through 3, you'll also get familiar with the sport and the jargon, learn how to set relevant goals, and get set up with all the right tri gear.

The nuts and bolts of training are detailed in part II of the book. We'll tackle swimming, biking, and running in chapters 4 through 6, then show you how to integrate all three in chapter 7. And because some consider transitions to be a sport in itself (although I've seen transitions more akin to slapstick comedy), we'll cover training tips to teach you to go from one sport to the next without missing a beat.

In part III, we'll cover all you need to know to stay on track. In chapter 8, you'll find some fundamentals of sports nutrition, and you'll avoid the dreaded injury bug by reading chapter 9 before that next killer workout. Chapter 10 will provide you with all the practical considerations you need to think about before that big race. For the second edition, we've added a new chapter 11 that focuses entirely on race day, giving you everything you need to know—from prerace considerations to what to eat during an event to postrace analysis. Finally, chapter 12 will pave the way for you to make triathlon not just a new sport for you, but a healthy, fun, and wonderfully gratifying way of life.

Need some inspiration and motivation? I've interviewed dozens of triathletes—both amateurs and professionals—about their early triathlon experience, and included the most interesting, funny, and inspiring success stories from the lot. The second edition features some new faces and inspiring stories.

You'll find plenty of useful tools here too, such as checklists, tips, examples, and the additional resources you need to learn the sport of triathlon or take your triathlon experience to that next level. With all these handy tools, you'll find *Triathlon 101* a practical workbook you can use on every step of your multisport adventure.

This new edition of *Triathlon 101* is retooled to address the latest equipment advances, new training techniques, and growing trends. We've also updated this second edition with the latest scientific research on fitness, nutrition, and performance, such as running in the heat.

You'll find other helpful updates as well throughout. For example, if you're a later bloomer and jumping on the triathlon bandwagon a little late in life, chapter 1 addresses training considerations that will make your journey safe and fulfilling.

Triathlon 101 is your first and best step to training for, and racing, your first triathlon. When you take it one step at a time, it makes every subsequent step more enjoyable and rewarding. I hope this enhanced book will give you everything you need on your first race day, and for many finish lines beyond.

Acknowledgments

I'd like to acknowledge the following people for contributing their technical expertise to this book:

Terry Laughlin, for allowing me to use materials from his *Total Immersion* workbook and contributing an article that was adapted for use in the swim chapter. Lauren Jensen for her valuable tips in the cycling chapter. And Troy Jacobson for the expertise he's provided in the running chapter. For guidance on sports medicine topics, I'd like to thank: Dr. George Tsatsos, Dr. Lawrence Burns, Dr. Daryll Hobson, Dr. P. Michael Leahy, Lisa Alamar, Robert P. Nirschl, MD, and J.P. Neary, PhD.

For their input on topics regarding the sport of triathlon and equipment, thanks to: Bob Babbit, Jan Caille, Bob Langan, Dan Siever, Liz Downing, Steve Hed, Ken Souza, John Cobb, and Dan Empfield.

Many thanks to the profiled triathletes who let us peek into their own unique experience, and in the process, gave us all the gift of inspiration: Chris Lieto, Joseph Picciuca, Mike Greer, Marti Greer, Amanda Stevens, Michellie Jones, Joe Albert, Ben Holliss, Dion Harrison, Toby Baxendale, Christian Racoma, and Bernard Lyles.

Other people that contributed in various aspects of putting the book together: Jeffrey Justice, former (and best ever) editor of *Triathlete Magazine*—wherever you are. Shelley Berryhill, former editor of *Windy City Sports* for assigning me all those triathlon articles, as well as Jeff Banowitz, who continues to do the same. And Anne Hall and Laurel Plotzke at Human Kinetics for keeping me honest.

Most of all, thanks to Linda, for her support and love.

PART I

Getting Ready to Tri

Preparation is the key to your successful introduction into multisports. From knowing what distances to choose, to setting a goal, to buying the right equipment, your experience will go much more smoothly if you make the effort to prepare before you start to train. The next few chapters will help you do that.

chapter 1

So You Wanna Tri?

*Life is a positive-sum game. . . . Everyone from the gold medal-
ist to the last finisher can rejoice in a personal victory.*

—George Sheehan

Remember when you were a kid? Think back for a minute and remember a time that was simpler, less worrisome, and, well, more fun. Think about how you used to play: chasing your friends, pedaling your first bike, going to the beach. Hear your friends shouting, "Let's jump in the pool! Let's go bike riding! Race you to the corner!"

In a sense, we all grew up as triathletes. Sure, we may not have swum, biked, and run in that order or traversed any significant distances, but we knew the fun of mixing things up a bit. For playful, energetic children who craved fun, running, cycling, and swimming were three common summertime activities.

Everybody has his or her unique motivation for getting involved in a new activity, but I've always felt that one of the greatest lures of the multi-sport world is the sheer enjoyment of combining three different and challenging physical activities into one exciting sport.

The Sport for the Rest of Us

During a recent beginners' triathlon seminar put on by the Chicago Triathlon Club, a revelation hit me as I looked at those assembled. The attendees were no longer frustrated runners, limping to the triathlon to relieve their overstressed ligaments. Nor were they prune-skin swimmers, tired of following the black line at the bottom of the pool. Pedal-happy cyclists looking for a new reason to shave their legs? Nope.

Most of the attendants were true newcomers to the sport, many with little athletic background or training knowledge. They were the homemaker who never even ran a 10K, the construction worker who could barely swim one pool length, and the nurse who hadn't been on her Schwinn since high school. All of them were eager to become active participants in multisports, achieve fitness, and find personal satisfaction in doing triathlons.

More and more people today—regardless of their background or athletic talent—are interested in total fitness. The type of person who seeks to become a triathlete nowadays is, on average, just that—an average person wanting to achieve something extraordinary in his or her life. Sometimes there's a specific motivation—a life turn or wake-up call to embrace a healthier, fitter lifestyle. No matter where you've come from and why you're seeking to "tri" all three, triathlon is the ideal sport of the new millennium for many reasons.

An Outdoor Experience

Triathlons give you the refreshing, invigorating feeling of swimming in a lake or ocean, cycling on roads that take you through striking countryside scenery, and running on a pristine trail or path. How else can you experience nature in three distinct ways, all in the span of a few hours? Granted, not all triathlon venues are located in national or state parks. Sometimes the scenery from the bike consists entirely of metal skyscrapers. Still, with the exception of indoor multisport events and big-city races, the great outdoors makes the triathlon a feast for the senses and a welcome respite from urban blight.

Variety Is the Spice of Multisport

If you've ever trained for a single sport event, such as a marathon or a long bike ride, then you know how monotonous training can get. Multisport training brings variety back to your workout routine. The simple act of doing a different workout each day will be a real lift to your body, mind, and spirit. The variety will also increase the odds that you stay on track and reap the many health benefits of triathlon, such as increased fitness, better health, and a more active lifestyle.

Tri-ing Puts the Fun Back in Fitness

For many people, fitness is drudgery. It's a daily or weekly chore, something that has to be done on a regular basis, like cleaning the house, mowing the lawn, or paying the bills. You see it all the time in health clubs—frustrated men and women who monotonously and joylessly push themselves on stationary machines for the sole purpose of burning calories or shaving those love handles. They never look like they're having fun, which is probably why most New Year's fitness resolutions don't last past the first day of spring.

Exercise doesn't have to be that way. Yes, exercise can be fun, especially when you have three sports to work with. Sure, you'll have to work hard and get your heart rate up, but who says it has to be drudgery? If part of your purpose in pursuing multisports is losing weight and getting into shape, that's OK. Just try to keep it lighthearted, and you might find that you'll achieve your goals regarding weight or physique without feeling like you're mopping the kitchen floor.

Success Through Working on Weaknesses

Robert Kratzke/Icon SMI

Simply put, Michellie Jones is one of the best triathletes in the world, male or female. With wins at every distance, over a huge variety of courses, and against world-class competition, Jones has proven herself time and time again when it counts.

The Australian triathlete has an athleticism and competitiveness that were nurtured at an early age . . . you could even say it's in her genes. Since birth, she's had friendly rivalries with her twin sister.

It was her high school running coach who first suggested she compete in triathlons in 1998. So she gave it a try in a sprint-distance race and ended up placing second overall and winning her age group, even though she had very little swimming experience and lacked top-level equipment. "I remember that I rode with a $200 bike and rode in my running shoes with no aerobars."

Bitten by the triathlon bug and her initial success, she set out to improve her swimming and cycling. She then went on to compete in a growing Australian racing circuit, and she paid her way through college with her winnings. In 1991 she came to the United States and began a legendary career as a pro triathlete.

To date, Michellie has 160 wins under her belt and counting, including the Ironman, a silver medal in the 2000 Sydney Olympics, 12 World Cup victories, 8 ITU world championship medals, and scores of wins in some of the sport's most prestigious events.

"I think what drove me early on was my drive to get better and better in the pool and on the bike. Once I found a sport that I truly loved, it was really strong motivation and a challenge to work on my weaknesses."

Besides working on weakness, Michellie emphasizes the need to set goals: "For beginners, the most important thing is to have a major goal, such as finishing your first triathlon, based on minigoals for training. These could be swimming in open water, running continuously for 5K, or riding a set distance. And setting your major goal, maybe even registering for a race you want to complete, will keep you honest. You know you have to be ready on that race day, so that will keep you motivated and working on your minigoals."

It's a Better Balancing Act

One of the keys to success in multisport training is striking just the right balance. You'll have to become proficient at juggling types of workouts, intensity, distance, and other factors, in addition to balancing the time devoted to all three sports. To be sure, you'll need to learn from experience; trial and error are definitely part of the equation. But the skills you learn from balancing your multisport training can translate directly into the rest of your life in many positive ways. From learning to balance several activities or priorities at once, to effective time management, you're sure to reap the rewards in other areas of your life away from athletics.

Three's a Challenge

Although marathoning is certainly a formidable test of endurance, triathlons have now become a good alternative for the pavement-weary warrior. Triathlon training requires disciplined workouts in three different sports, and triathletes who delve into half-Ironman distance or Ironman territory must tackle significant training and have tons of self-discipline to achieve their goals. Although you may not be setting your sights on the Hawaii Ironman Triathlon right now, completing any distance in triathlon is still a formidable task.

Three's a Cinch

On the other hand, training for a short-distance triathlon is a lot easier than training for a marathon, at least in terms of total workout time. I don't mean to imply that completing your first triathlon will be a piece of cake. If you're deathly afraid of water, learning to swim may be the hardest thing you do in your life. Or if you've let yourself get out of shape, running more than a few minutes may be a big challenge. Yet a short-distance triathlon that might take you 90 minutes is certainly a more manageable goal than a 26.2-mile foot race that might take you 4 or 5 hours.

It's a Group Effort

You're not alone in your aspirations to be a totally fit triathlete. Triathlon clubs, magazines, national organizations, Web sites, and training groups are all resources that you can tap into. In particular, local clubs are a great way to learn about the sport and meet people to train with. Sure, triathlon isn't as popular in the mainstream as, say, running or cycling, but if you look hard enough, you'll probably find your ideal training partner or group. Even if you prefer the peacefulness of of training on your own, as many runners and cyclists do, it's always nice to know that there are group activities you can participate in when you feel the need to be more social.

Triathlon: Where Did It Come From?

Perhaps your exposure to triathlon came through a friend or by watching the famous Ironman Triathlon in Hawaii on television. Unless you've been around triathlon for a long time, you're probably curious about the history of the sport.

The first true multisport event was a biathlon (now called duathlon, so the name doesn't conflict with the run-and-rifle sport). Although many people have the misconception that the Hawaii Ironman was the first triathlon, the first true triathlon was a lot shorter than the grueling race you may have seen on television. The following section is a rundown of the origins of the sport that you're about to jump into.

Triathlon Time Line

The modern version of triathlon had its roots in duathlon, progressed to a three-sport event, and has evolved into a worldwide phenomenon.

Early history: According to triathlon historian and author Scott Tinley, the origin of triathlon is anecdotally attributed to a race in France in the 1920s or 1930s that was called Les Trois Sports (The Three Sports). This race consists of a 3K run, 12K bike, and a crossing of the channel Marne.

1972: San Diego lawyer David Pain, one of the founders of the masters running movement in the United States, puts on the David Pain Birthday Biathlon, consisting of a 10K run and a half-mile swim.

1974: Two members of the San Diego Track Club add a bike ride to the mix and put on the first true triathlon, held on Fiesta Island near the present-day Sea World. The Mission Bay Triathlon consists of a 2.8-mile run, a 5-mile bike ride, a .25-mile swim, a 2-mile run, and a .25-mile swim.

1977: Tired of swimmers and cyclists arguing with him and his running friends about who was the better athlete, Navy commander John Collins challenges a crowd gathered at the awards party for the Oahu running relay race to go beyond a single sport. The gauntlet he threw down? Complete three separate events all in one day: the 2.4-mile Waikiki Rough Water Swim, the 115-mile Around-the-Island Bike Ride, and the 26.2-mile Honolulu Marathon. Whoever could win such a race, he announces, could call himself (no women raced the first year) an iron man.

1978: After a year's preparation by John Collins, the first Ironman Triathlon is held on February 18, 1978. Fifteen men, including Collins, race on that day. The first Ironman champion is a former Navy pentathlete, Gordon Haller.

1982: Word spreads about the Ironman, courtesy of *Sports Illustrated* and ABC Sports. Millions of television viewers witness the famous 400-yard crawl of courageous triathlete Julie Moss at the finish line, putting the sport of triathlon on the media map. That same year, the United States Triathlon Series is created, bringing shorter distance races to the mainstream and paving the way for future growth.

1989: The first Triathlon World Championship is held in Avignon, France, using the Olympic distance (also known as the International distance) of a 1.5K swim, a 40K bike, and a 10K run.

2000: Triathlon joins the Olympic Games as a full medal sport in Sydney, Australia. Appropriately, the event distance chosen for this inaugural event is the Olympic distance.

The Sport of Triathlon Today

The preceding time line is a short history of some events that shaped the beginnings of the triathlon. Other major events, such as the creation of the sport's U.S. governing body, Tri-Fed, now known as USA Triathlon, and the introduction of bicycle aerobars, have a lot to do with the sport as it is today.

Triathlete legends and pioneers in the early days, such as the Big Four—Dave Scott, Scott Molina, Scott Tinley, and Mark Allen—as well as female trailblazers Erin Baker, Paula Newby-Fraser, Colleen Cannon, and Julie Moss, paved the way for future generations of professional triathletes. More important, they brought big-time media attention to a very small sport, thus bringing triathlon to people who were getting tired of running marathon after marathon.

Better Late Than Never

If you think that triathlon is a young person's sport, all you need to do is go to any local multisport event to change your mind. At most triathlons, particularly the larger ones, you can see throngs of older men and women splashing, mashing, and dashing their way through the course with the exuberance of a playground toddler.

If you're considering taking on triathlon for the first time and you're well into your 40s, 50s, 60s, or beyond, you certainly won't be alone in your age group. And although you should enter any new endurance activity with a degree of caution, especially as you get older, there are many benefits triathlon has to offer the more seasoned novice:

- An Italian study of endurance athletes and triathletes with an average age of 63 showed that their blood vessels functioned as well as those of 27-year-olds (Taddei 2000).
- The same study also showed that older triathletes had significantly low blood levels of free radicals, which may help slow the aging process.
- Cross-training can help older athletes avoid injuries that they may be more susceptible to, such as those from high-impact activities like marathon training.
- Exercise can reduce the pain caused by arthritis.
- According to USA Triathlon's membership figures for 2007, more than 36 percent of their members are over the age of 40, so you won't be alone! (www.usatriathlon.org/content/index/817)

Special Considerations for the Older Tri-Geek

While the benefits of triathlon training and racing are numerous for older triathletes, the decision to move forward in the sport should also be weighed against the risks.

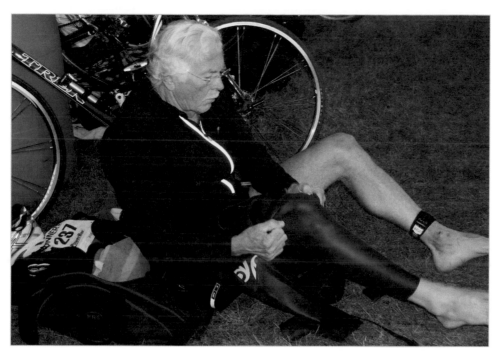

The cross-training involved in triathlon is beneficial to older athletes in preventing certain types of sports injuries.

"It's important to get a complete physical examination, because triathlon training does put a significant amount of stress on the cardiovascular system for older people, especially if they haven't participated in endurance sports before," says Dr. Jeffrey Sankoff, MD, two-time Ironman triathlete and ER physician who is in his mid-40s. "You also have to consider that you don't have the body of a 20-year-old, which means that your recovery time is going to be longer. That requires a certain amount of patience and the forethought to build in more rest or easy days into your schedule," adds Sankoff. Nevertheless, triathlon's multisport balancing act is ideal for both the body and mind of an older triathlete. Providing you take the proper precaution, jumping into triathlon late in life will ignite a passion that is sure to keep you young of heart, literally and figuratively.

Recovering and Avoiding Injury Over 40

If you are over 40, here are tips in three areas that should help you recover from training faster and keep you injury-free.

- **Flexibility.** Devote time to stretching, particularly after training when your muscles and ligaments are warmed up and more pliable. As you get older, flexibility decreases, making it more likely that you'll pull or strain something. Do all you can to offset this reduction; for example, consider adding yoga to your training routine.

- **Strength training.** It's critical to perform 30 minutes of resistance training at least three times per week. This is particularly helpful for women in preventing debilitating conditions such as osteoporosis and osteoarthritis, which often come on later in life.
- **Equipment.** Choose the right gear and get a properly fitted bicycle. You can easily injure yourself by having your bicycle saddle too low or running in the wrong running shoes. Of course, that is true for everyone, but doubly so when your seasoned muscles and joints are less resilient to the strain and stress of training with ill-chosen or poorly set-up equipment.

Your Triathlon Choices

Now that you know more about triathlon's history than many tri veterans, it's a good time to talk about the variety of multisport event distances you have to choose from. Unlike some sports with very strict format guidelines, virtually any event that includes a swim, a bike ride, and a run can be called a triathlon.

There are indoor triathlons, triathlons that start with a swim and end with a swim, triathlons that have two bike legs, and mountain bike triathlons with the run and the bike held on trails, to name just a few. The triathlon is limited only by the venue and the imagination of the race director. Even though there are many unique events that deviate from the traditional, the swim-bike-run format is the most prevalent and, in all likelihood, is the kind of event that has seized your interest.

In terms of distance, again, the sky's the limit. Most triathlons, however, do fall under one of four distance categories. (You'll probably find plenty of races that fall somewhere in between these distances, which is part of what makes triathlon unique.) The following sections describe each of the four predominant distances and provide recommendations to give you an idea of where you might want to set your sights.

Sprint Distance: .75K Swim, 20K Bike Ride, and 5K Run

The trend today is toward more short-distance races; at present over 50 percent of all triathlons are the sprint distance. In the sport's infancy, the longer distances and the "gruel-a-thon" image gave triathlon a certain degree of novelty, but now the reality is that there is a greater demand for more manageable events.

A case in point is the Carlsbad Triathlon. A popular California event, it began to see its participation numbers decline a few years ago, from 1,000 to under 700. The race directors decided to change from the Olympic distance to a sprint distance and the numbers quickly climbed back up over 1,000. "There are just many more people that don't have the time to train for a two-hour event, but can manage a one-hour race," says Bob Babbit, triathlon guru and publisher of *Competitor Magazine*. "Shorter events really fill up."

TRIATHLON FACTS

History shows that although triathlon has experienced growing pains and political infighting—the kind of stuff that happens in any organized sport—multisport events are here to stay. Need proof? Here are a few facts:

Fact: Since 1980, triathlon has been one of the fastest-growing recreational sports in the United States. According to USA Triathlon, their membership reached the 100,000-member milestone in 2007: 200,000 to 250,000 athletes compete every year in the United States alone.

Fact: On an international level, triathlon is booming. In Australia, triathlon is taught as a sport at the high school level, and organized swim-bike-run competitions are commonplace between schools.

Fact: Over 50 percent of all triathlons are sprint distance, a very short race that requires a minimum of training. So triathlon, once perceived to be the exclusive domain of superathletes, has become a mainstream sport with options to suit every lifestyle and level of commitment.

Fact: Triathlon race directors report continued increases in participation. The Wildflower Triathlon, held annually at Lake San Antonio, California, for over 25 years, boasted over 5,400 participants for their 2005 race.

Fact: NBC's prime-time Olympic coverage showed very high viewer ratings during coverage of the women's Olympic triathlon in 2004—it was seen in 24.3 million American households, according to Nielsen Media Research.

Fact: International Triathlon Union World Cup and Ironman races are shown on the Outdoor Life Network. The Ironman World Championship is shown yearly on NBC, whose coverage of the event has won numerous Emmys.

Sprint-distance races are ideal for the following people:

- Beginning triathletes who want to jump in and catch the multisport bug
- Hares who lose their energy in races lasting over 90 minutes
- Level-headed types who have neither the desire nor the inclination to press the endurance envelope
- Time-pressed triathletes who don't have more than 10 hours a week to train for longer-distance races
- Triathletes who want to go fast the whole way
- Triathletes willing to commit to three to four months of consistent training

Olympic Distance: 1.5K Swim, 40K Bike Ride, 10K Run

The Olympic distance was popularized by the United States Triathlon Series, also known as the Bud Light races, during the '80s. This distance was instrumental in bringing triathlon to the mainstream. Even though it might take the average person close to three hours to complete, the Olympic distance, then called the "middle" distance, was a way to participate in a new and exciting sport without traveling to Hawaii and racing on the lava fields all day. As its name implies, this distance is also the distance triathletes from around the world race at the Olympics.

The Olympic distance is ideal for those who wish to push the endurance envelope beyond the two-hour boundary. If you're looking for a definite challenge and are not quite ready for a longer-course triathlon, training for an Olympic-distance event can help you get into great shape.

Olympic-distance races are ideal for the following people:

- Newcomers to the sport who already have a solid endurance base in an aerobic sport
- Experienced cyclists who occasionally run
- Veteran runners who occasionally bike
- Swimmers who plan on doing a lot more biking and running
- Triathletes who are willing to commit to 10 to 15 hours of training per week
- Triathletes willing to commit to five to six months of consistent training

Half-Ironman Distance: 1.2-Mile Swim, 56-Mile Bike Ride, 13.1-Mile Run

Half-Ironman races represent a serious level of competition for triathletes looking to expand their endurance horizons. Whereas you might be able to eke out a sprint- or maybe even an Olympic-distance race on minimal training, half-Ironman distances will make you regret any less-than-serious commitment to training long before you finish your race.

Half-Ironman races are a hotbed of age-group competition, and many of these events are Ironman qualifiers (which means you get a chance to race in Hawaii if you're fast enough). Although you might be used to seeing quite a few weekend warriors rolling in on their mountain bikes or Schwinn La Tours at sprint-, or maybe even Olympic-distance races, you'll be hard pressed to find anybody who hasn't plunked down a few grand on a sleek and super lightweight tri-machine at these events.

Don't be intimidated by this difference if you prefer the long haul and are willing to swim, bike, and run for five hours or more. Nobody says you can't still do it on your fat-tire machine or cruiser (I've seen many people have a great time at these events on their old clunkers). Just don't expect any bagels to be left at the finish line for you.

Half-Ironman races are ideal for the following people:

- Triathletes with at least one year's experience racing sprint- or Olympic-distance events

- Endurance cyclists with some running experience
- Runners with several half-marathons under their belts and some cycling experience
- Swimmers who plan on doing more biking and running than they'd like to think about
- Triathletes who are willing to commit to 15 to 20 hours of training per week
- Triathletes willing to commit to six to nine months of consistent training.

Ironman Distance: 2.4-Mile Swim, 112-Mile Bike Ride, 26.2-Mile Run

The Ultimate. The Big Show. The Big Hurt. What else can you say about the holy grail of triathlon? (OK, technically, the Ironman Triathlon in Hawaii is the real holy grail of the sport, but I think anybody who does any race of this distance should be considered a Sir or Lady Galahad.) Some triathletes train for years to get to the point where they can traverse these distances without going into a coma.

Needless to say (but I'll say it anyway), the challenge of training and racing an Ironman-distance race should not be entered into lightly. Completing an Ironman safely requires an enormous amount of preparation and commitment. Some triathletes race an entire lifetime without completing this distance, either by design or because the time commitments are too great. Training for an Ironman may also put some emotional strain on your family and interfere with your career.

WHAT'S AN IRONMAN QUALIFIER?

If you've been reading the race section of your favorite multisport magazine, or been hanging around triathlon veterans, the phrase *Ironman qualifier* might have popped out at you. The phrase refers to one of the only two ways a triathlete is allowed to race in the Ironman Triathlon in Hawaii. Because the race is so popular and only a limited number of participants are allowed for safety reasons, event officials had to find a fair way to allow only the best triathletes to race in the sweltering heat and blustery winds of the island of Kona. Therefore, a limited number of established races are designated every year as Ironman qualifiers. These races are held around the world and range in length from Olympic-distance to Ironman-distance races. Participants who finish at the top of their age group in these events are awarded an Ironman slot, which allows them to enter the Big Show. Oh, and for us speed-challenged triathletes, there's still hope. A very limited number of Ironman slots (usually 50) are allocated in a lottery drawing, which anybody can get in on (for a fee).

Triathlon—the events.

Although it may seem as though I'm trying to discourage you from setting your sights on an Ironman, I am not. It is the ultimate triathlon event, and I believe the crowning achievement for any experienced triathlete who wishes to reach a landmark in his or her multisport career. The key word in that previous sentence is *experienced*. A newcomer to the sport, however eager, should think twice, or three or four times, before sending in an application for an Ironman event. Earn your stripes in other distances for at least a year. Then you can go for the Big One.

Ironman-distance races are ideal for the following people:

- Triathletes who have completed several half-Ironman events and plan to increase their training to that next level
- Veteran triathletes who are looking for the ultimate challenge
- Triathletes who are willing to commit to 20 to 30 hours of training per week, possibly more
- Triathletes who are willing to commit to a year of consistent training.

Tri-ing It Indoors

A great option for winter-bound triathletes or novices who fear open water is the indoor triathlon. Some indoor events keep all three activities inside: The bike leg is done on a stationary machine and the running portion on an indoor track or treadmill. Many indoor triathlons hold only the swimming portion in an indoor pool, and the bike and the run are held outside.

Indoor events also make great first triathlons and are a good way of starting off a triathlon season. They tend to be less intimidating because of the pool swim. Indoor events usually have few participants and are short in length (they normally don't go beyond the sprint distance).

Another Choice: The Triathlon Relay

Relay competition has become an increasingly popular offshoot of triathlon. Teams consist of a swimmer, a cyclist, and a runner who compete against other teams for the best total time. Many teams come close to bettering the professional finishing times. For many, team participation gives them a chance to have fun, improve fitness, and delve into the exciting world of multisport athletics without the full triathlon training schedule. For future triathletes, it provides a stepping-stone to the full distance.

For many active people who train regularly in one discipline, relaying offers a comfortable vantage point from which to view triathlon fever. Although not every triathlon includes a relay competition, for the large events the relay has become a door by which those who want to feel out triathlons, those who thrive on team competition, and those with limitations can participate in an exciting multisport event. Among other advantages of relay divisions, they bring the spirit of team competition to an individual sport. Finally, relays are a means by which those who may think they could never do a triathlon might reconsider.

Let's Get Started!

Now that you've got an overview of triathlon's multiple sports and some your racing options, it's time to start planning for races, choosing the right equipment, and, of course, training. In the next eleven chapters, we'll cover all the basics you need to finish your first triathlon safely—and with a satisfying grin spread across your face. Let's get started!

chapter 2

Planning to Race

I always wanted to be somebody, but I should have been more specific.

—Lily Tomlin

Although most people enter multisports with the purpose of completing several triathlons, there are those who finish one and hang up their swim caps forever. They continue to cross-train, but they feel no need to compete against others or to better a personal best. But if, like me, you love to race, then it's important to create a plan. Your goal can be anything, such as achieving a personal best or consistently training six days out of the week. However, setting your triathlon beacon on a race—whether it be a relay, sprint, or Olympic-distance event—will help you narrow your focus for a successful and satisfying experience.

Now that you have an idea of your triathlon choices, are you ready to set your sights on a particular race and make a plan? This chapter is interactive, with lots of questions and exercises that will help you make wise decisions. You'll need to sharpen your pencil because you'll fill in some blanks and do some writing. It'll be worth the effort—the answers you provide will lay the foundation for your triathlon adventure.

Step 1: Take a Personal Inventory

The distance you choose will depend on your current fitness level, your experience with other sports, and your comfort level with open-water swimming. Even if you've got your first triathlon under your belt and are looking to go faster or longer, you'll still need to carefully consider these planning issues. Take stock of your fitness and skills by answering a few simple questions in the following worksheets.

What Is My Cardiorespiratory Fitness Level?

This question is one worth taking some time to evaluate. To get where you want to go, you must first know where you are. By honestly evaluating your current fitness level, you avoid putting undue pressure on yourself by setting your initial sights too high. Putting pressure on yourself usually leads to injury from increasing mileage or intensity (or both) too quickly.

If you need to get in a lot of running and cycling, why not enjoy building an endurance base by taking your time, gradually increasing your distance, and maybe even doing a few running or cycling races in the meantime? It might take a little longer, but you'll find that by first honestly assessing your current fitness, you can create a training plan that is safe, systematic, and enjoyable. To help you gauge where you stand, photocopy and complete the Cardiorespiratory Fitness Worksheet.

Cardiorespiratory Fitness Worksheet

Number of times per week you engage in aerobic exercise:	
Number of months you've maintained this exercise routine:	
Rate your current cardiorespiratory fitness level on a scale of 1 to 10 (10 being the most fit).	

From J. Mora, 2009, *Triathlon 101*, 2nd ed. (Champaign, IL: Human Kinetics).

How Are My Swimming Skills?

The nice thing about running and cycling is that neither takes the grace or coordination of a ballerina or the sensory skills of a marksman. So, in most cases, the only skill that really requires polishing is front-crawl swimming, an activity that requires some technical competence. (If the swim is very short, you can get by with a breaststroke or sidestroke—but I wouldn't recommend it because both of these strokes are very inefficient.)

If your swimming skills are not quite up to par, don't feel left out. Many triathletes don't swim like fish. Still, those who are serious about jumping into the sport and sticking around for a while commit to improving, developing, or, in many cases, just learning to swim in the first place. For beginners, a local city college or YMCA program is a great place to start. If your swimming needs some serious work and it's already the middle of the triathlon racing season, why not set a target for next year and take beginning or intermediate swimming classes during the fall and winter months? You could compete in duathlons for now and concentrate on getting ready for triathlon next year.

You should also assess your comfort level in open water. Does that thought send a shiver down your spine? Well, again, you're not alone. Newcomers to the sport often find open-water swimming unnerving. If you're one of the many who feel like fish out of water in open water, then learning to swim in a lake or ocean might be your biggest challenge (unless your only triathlon aspiration is to complete an indoor triathlon). Part II of this book covers open-water swimming in greater detail. For now, try to gauge where you currently stand (or tread water) by completing the Swimming Skills Worksheet and the Open-Water Swimming Worksheet below.

Swimming Skills Worksheet

Can you swim the front crawl across a full pool length without stopping? (circle one)	**Yes No**
If yes, write the number of pool lengths you can currently complete without stopping:	
Rate your skills in the front crawl on a 1 to 10 scale. For example, if you find yourself unable to submerge your head while swimming, a realistic assessment might be 1. If you have a basic understanding of proper technique but have poor execution, rate yourself a 5. If your execution is fair to excellent, give yourself a number between 6 and 10.	

From J. Mora, 2009, *Triathlon 101*, 2nd ed. (Champaign, IL: Human Kinetics).

Open-Water Worksheet

Have you ever swum in open water before?	**Yes**	**No**

Which statement best describes your comfort level in open water? (check one)

____ My middle name is Flipper   ____ Mildly uncomfortable

____ Pretty comfortable   ____ Extremely uncomfortable

____ OK

From J. Mora, 2009, *Triathlon 101*, 2nd ed. (Champaign, IL: Human Kinetics).

How Is My Cycling Ability?

Unless you come from a road racing background, it's likely that the only experience you have in cycling is recreational. We'll tackle some specific ways you can learn the technical skills to handle yourself behind the handlebars of triathlon bicycle (or mountain bike, if you happen to be training for an XTERRA off-road triathlon), but for now, assess some key aspects of your cycling fitness using the following worksheet.

Cycling Ability Worksheet

Do you have any experience riding a thin-tire road bike on a road?	Yes	No
If yes, do you ride on a regular basis?	Yes	No
Do you participate in group cycling rides or belong to a cycling club?	Yes	No
What is the longest you've ridden on a bicycle? (measured in time or distance)		
Are there any previous injuries or physical conditions that would make it difficult to participate in cycling training?	Yes	No

From J. Mora, 2009, *Triathlon 101*, 2nd ed. (Champaign, IL: Human Kinetics).

How Is My Running Ability?

Most people who are thinking about doing their first triathlon have some experience with running, even if it's just an occasional jog. Use the following worksheet to evaluate your current running abilities as well as other factors that will help determine how well you transition into run training for triathlon.

Running Ability Worksheet

Have you participated in any running event, such as 5Ks, 10Ks, or marathons?	Yes	No
If yes, how many?		
Do you participate in organized training runs or belong to a running club?	Yes	No
What is the longest you've run? (measured in time or distance)		
Are there any previous injuries or physical conditions that would make it difficult to participate in run training?	Yes	No

From J. Mora, 2009, *Triathlon 101*, 2nd ed. (Champaign, IL: Human Kinetics).

Step 2: Set a Realistic Goal

Have you ever started to work toward something only to find that you didn't have the time, energy, or motivation to complete your goal? Or worse, have you ever exhausted yourself physically, mentally, and spiritually to accomplish a goal, only to realize that you didn't enjoy getting there?

If you want to succeed in the multisport arena, you've got to set a realistic goal. Now, "realistic" is different for everyone; what might be realistic for one person is totally insane for somebody else. All of us have unique responsibilities in terms of work, family, and community. The trick is to determine a commitment level that will contribute to a balanced lifestyle and not cause stress.

You might set multiple goals; if you do, the more focused you are, the better your chances. For example, you might have specific times you'd like to finish each leg of a triathlon in, as well as a finishing time. There's nothing wrong with having multiple goals, as long as you are realistic about your time and capabilities. For now, though, why not focus on one chief goal? With that in mind, let's move through a few questions that will help determine what that goal will be.

What Distance Is Right for Me?

Keeping in mind your current fitness level, refer to chapter 1 and reread the descriptions of the four predominant distance categories. Don't make the mistake of setting your race goal too high above your current fitness level, especially if your base training has been minimal. (*Base training* is a term covered later in the training chapters. For now, understand that this term describes a fitness foundation of regular aerobic exercise in an endurance sport over an extended period.)

A Late Bloomer

Whoever said you can't teach an old dog new tricks never met Mike Greer. A highly successful businessman, triathlon race director, and book author, Mike completed his first triathlon in 1984 at the age of 44. But long before he crossed his first triathlon finish line, Mike took stock of his skills and realized he needed to put in some serious swimming and cycling time. Because he was a veteran marathoner, his cardiorespiratory fitness and running base were solid. Yet his swimming and cycling were serious weaknesses.

Courtesy of Mike Greer.

"I began to swim a lot because I had the endurance, but in hindsight, I should have found a coach to help me with my technique," says the 70-year-old resident of Lubbock, Texas. "I read everything on swimming and cycling I could get my hands on and visited the local bike shops for advice on equipment and gearing. I spent a lot of time with other swimmers, cyclists, and triathletes, learning everything I could from them." With this commonsense approach to improving on the skills he was lacking, he completed his first triathlon after a year of training.

Since then, he has become heavily involved in the sport's political arena and is the race director of the popular Buffalo Springs Lake Triathlon, a half-Ironman event in Lubbock, as well as several other events, including a women's race series. He currently has 308 triathlon finishes to his credit, including 7 Ironman-distance races. "I'm slow, painfully slow, but I can keep going," Mike says of his race times. "I love triathlon, the people, and the lifestyle. It's a helluva deal."

Are you willing to put in the training that is required before attempting a sprint- or Olympic-distance triathlon? If not, what about a relay? If you have a specific race coming up soon that you're thinking of doing, do you have enough time to train? For example, if you come from a running background, but your longest run thus far has been six miles, and your cycling and swimming have been nil, the half-Ironman triathlon next month is not realistic.

Besides your current fitness, consider how much time you have to train, how training will affect your family life, career, or both.

Although a sprint distance requires a relatively small amount of training, training for an Ironman can be like taking on another full-time job. Complete the Distance Worksheet to determine which triathlon distance best suits you now.

Distance Worksheet

Approximate number of hours per week you can commit to triathlon training: _____

What triathlon distance is right for you, based on training times given in chapter 1? (check one)

____ Relay   ____ Half Ironman*

____ Sprint   ____ Ironman*

____ Olympic

*If one of these distances is your choice, be sure to consider the effect on your family life, career, etc.

From J. Mora, 2009, *Triathlon 101*, 2nd ed. (Champaign, IL: Human Kinetics).

Which Race Should I Do?

Now comes the moment for you to put it all on the line and choose a specific race as your triathlon goal. Check multisport publications and the Internet for races in your area. Ask your triathlete friends which races they would recommend. Ideally, you should be looking for a race that gives you ample time to get up to speed, depending on the inventory you took in step 1. Don't plan for a race that will rush your training. If it's already late in the triathlon racing season, plan for next season.

Look for the following information when reviewing races:

- Number of years the race has been around
- USA Triathlon–sanctioned, or sanctioned by your triathlon national governing body if you live outside the United States (not a necessity, but the top races usually are)
- What your triathlon friends (the ones who have done the race) say about it
- Safety of the swim course, such as the number of lifeguards and how clearly you can see the swim buoys

- Aid stations on the run course (and on the bike course for Olympic distances or longer)
- Race application fee
- Postrace food and activities
- Available lodging and accommodations in the race area (if staying overnight)
- Whether the race is at sea level or high altitude, for possible acclimation issues

If you're new to the sport, keep things as simple as possible for your first few races. Local events within driving distance are better than having to deal with air travel and taking apart your bike to fit into a bicycle case. (The multisport air travel vacation might be a great getaway for the veteran, but it's not the best choice for the beginner.) Small races are better than circuslike mass starts, and rural venues can be less intimidating than metro madness.

Race Selection Worksheet

Taking into account my comfort level in open water and my swimming ability, I would prefer an

____ indoor swim   ____ open-water ocean swim

____ open-water lake swim

I would prefer a race

____ within driving distance ____ that I would travel to by air

I would prefer a

____ small race with fewer than 500 participants

____ a big race with more than 500 participants

I would prefer a race in

____ an urban setting   ____ a rural setting

My ideal bike and run course would be

____ flat as a pancake   ____ very hilly   ____ somewhat hilly   ____ off-road (e.g., XTERRA)

Given the preceding criteria, list a few races that you might be interested in doing.

1.

2.

3.

From the preceding list, which race takes place at a time of year that will give you the ideal amount of training time to ensure that you're fully prepared to complete the event?

Race name: _____

Race date: _____ Months to train: _____

From J. Mora, 2009, *Triathlon 101*, 2nd ed. (Champaign, IL: Human Kinetics).

Another variable to consider when selecting a race is whether you have a preference for off-road triathlons that feature a cycling leg comprised of a mountain bike course on a trail, such as the XTERRA Triathlon Series. If you're a novice triathlete who prefers the trail-riding experience or somebody with a mountain biking background, this type of race might be an ideal introduction to the sport. And, if you already have the right mountain bike and gear, it will save you money.

The Race Selection Worksheet on the previous page will help you narrow your choices.

What Do I Want to Accomplish?

There are three reasons to race: to finish, to improve, or to win. Unless you're a professional athlete or top age-grouper, your goal will likely be to finish or improve on previous finishing times. Ask yourself, "Is this a race I just want to finish, or am I willing to put in the necessary higher level of training to set a personal best?"

If your next triathlon will be your first ever, then it's best to set a goal of simply finishing. (If it's your first race, it'll be a personal best anyway, no matter what your finishing time, so you might as well just concentrate on finishing.) This approach takes a lot of pressure off yourself. You've got enough to worry about with your first race; don't create undue tension by demanding that you cross the finish line by a set time.

However, if you've done a triathlon or two and are looking to improve on your previous times, that's fine, too. The forthcoming chapters will provide you with all the information you need to get more familiar with the equipment and training techniques you need to bump up your speed or take on a longer distance. Fill out the Objectives Worksheet below to help provide focus to your plan.

Objectives Worksheet

What do I hope to accomplish?

_____ Finish the race

_____ Improve on a previous triathlon performance

      My previous triathlon performance: _____

_____ Win the race

      _____ Overall   _____ My age group

From J. Mora, 2009, *Triathlon 101*, 2nd ed. (Champaign, IL: Human Kinetics).

Why Do I Want to Do This Race?

Most people don't take the time to document their motivation behind a goal. They might create a training schedule or goal chart and proudly post it on their refrigerator door for all to see, but they don't bother to examine and write down the reason or reasons why they are embarking on this training program.

Making new friends and socializing can be great motivators as you embark upon triathlon training.

Goals, in themselves, are important. But if you don't have a clear idea of why you are setting those goals, you might find your motivation waning at critical junctures in your training (such as those cold and rainy mornings when you just don't feel like getting into the pool and practicing swim drills). Once you've committed yourself to a race goal, document—whether in a diary, journal, or triathlon training log—your true motivation in striving for this goal. (Marathon training logs are covered in more detail later.) Complete the motivation exercise on page 26, and then keep it where you will see it constantly, perhaps posted alongside your training schedule or list of goals on your refrigerator door.

GET FIRED UP! SAMPLE MOTIVATIONAL TIPS

- I'll improve my overall fitness by training and competing.
- I'll lose weight.
- I'll sleep better.
- I'll meet new and interesting people.
- I'll learn how to balance various activities.
- I'll become a better swimmer.
- Finishing a triathlon will give my self-confidence a boost.
- Even if I don't finish, I'll feel good about myself for having tried.
- It's a great excuse to buy a new bike!

Motivation Exercise

List 15 benefits of achieving your triathlon goal. Try to add 5 more to your list every week until you've reached 50.

1.
2.
3.
4.
5.
6.
7.
8.
9.
10.
11.
12.
13.
14.
15.

From J. Mora, 2009, *Triathlon 101*, 2nd ed. (Champaign, IL: Human Kinetics).

The above may seem like a lot, but motivational experts agree that the more firepower you have behind your goals, the more likely it is that you'll do the work and maintain the self-discipline you need to succeed. By listing the numerous benefits and reasons for desiring a goal, you'll build the motivational energy to get you through those tough training runs. I recommend 50 reasons as a minimum, but if you can stretch it to 100 reasons, you'll be so fired up, you won't be able to wait until your next swim, ride, or run.

Don't just look at the physical and external reasons. Point your emotional compass inward and analyze your feelings about this goal. One note: The longer your list, the harder this exercise becomes. But press on—usually it's those last few reasons that cut to the heart of your motivation.

Step 3: Set Up
Your Training Calendar and Log

Now that you know where you are and where you want to go, the final step is to get some things on paper (as if you haven't already worn out your pencil). Setting up your triathlon training calendar and log can be the two most important actions you take, perhaps more important than any swim intervals, long rides, or morning runs you do.

Individually Huff, Puff, and Tuff were no threat in a triathlon. But as a team . . .

Your Triathlon Training Calendar

Your training calendar can be a preprinted calendar, a poster board, an appointment book, or a calendar software program that prints out customized monthly grids. Just make sure that you have enough room to write down your daily workouts.

Your training calendar should also be on paper, as opposed to just on a computer screen. Although a software program is great for creating customized calendars, make sure it can print out monthly grids. You want your training calendar to be within plain sight, not hidden away somewhere on a computer hard drive. Dedicate a space for your calendar—someplace that you know you'll see every day. Once you've chosen your calendar and picked a place to put it, it's time to make the commitment and put pen to calendar (scary, huh?).

Work Your Way Back From Race Day

First, write your race goal on your training calendar. How much time does that give you to train properly? Again, take into account your current fitness level and skills. If you need to reassess your race goal and set your target on something more realistic, now is the time to do it.

Divide Your Calendar Into Phases

Although part II covers training in much more detail, you'll need to know a little bit about what experts consider to be the optimal way to train. Training in phases or cycles has long been considered the best way to condition the body to the rigors of endurance exercise. Each phase has a specific objective, and the workouts fulfill that objective.

Coaches and fitness experts don't always agree on the exact number of phases and objectives (largely because training differs among sports and elite athletes require more complex training plans). However, if you are a multisport novice or future triathlete looking for your first finish-line crossing, you should integrate some basic phases into your training calendar. Following is a brief description of each of these phases.

If you think you have a good handle on how much time you need to devote to each phase after reading this section, plan your training calendar accordingly. (Otherwise, wait until you review chapter 7 for more specific recommendations.) If you're superorganized, you might even want to use color highlighters to block off phases, using a different color for each one. Don't worry about writing down specific workouts; that comes later. For now, just get familiar with the phases, objectives, and estimated time frames.

Initiation Phase (Beginners Only)

Objective: Learn a new activity never or rarely performed before.

Estimated time: Depends on level of inexperience. If you are learning to swim the front crawl, this phase can take three months or more.

Base Phase

Objective: Create a foundation of training with gradual, safe adaptation to a physical activity.

Estimated time: Three to six months, depending on current conditioning, skills, and the distance for which you are training.

Speed and Technique Phase

Objective: Increase both the pace you can maintain and the efficiency of your exercise.

Estimated time: Three weeks to several months, depending on current conditioning and performance goals.

Race Simulation Phase

Objective: Boost race day confidence by completing workouts similar to what you will be doing in the event.

Estimated time: One to two months, depending on current conditioning and race goals.

Tapering Phase

Objective: Feel mentally and physically fresh for a race.

Estimated time: One to four weeks before your event, depending on the distance. Sprint-distance races usually only require a week of tapering.

Your Training Log

When you think of a journal or log, the first thought that might occur is sentimentality about the past. Part of the value of keeping such records is to remind you of your accomplishments, but keeping a record of your triathlon training and racing has more practical applications as well.

Training logs can help you avoid injuries and improve your performance. Maintaining an accurate log of your daily and weekly workouts is one of the best ways to keep on track. A log that chronicles the variables that affect your energy level and performance can help you achieve your triathlon goal.

You can purchase preprinted training logs. Some have motivating quotes and pictures and space for many variables. If you're a computer geek, several workout log programs are available.

There's no one way to keep a training log. Whatever you think are the most applicable variables are fine. Consider these variables for your own log:

- **Hours slept.** Current research suggests moderate sleep deprivation has little effect on performance during the adrenaline high of competition. Still, that ragged feeling during a three-mile training jog might be the result of too little snooze time.

- **Waking pulse.** Record your beats per minute when you awake, preferably while you're still in bed. An increase of more than three or four beats can signal overtraining.

- **Distances and times.** Tracking correct distances and workout times can keep you honest. It is also your most reliable measuring stick to check your progress.

- **Time of day.** Studies show that our energy levels fluctuate during the day. As long as all other variables remain the same, you can pinpoint your peak time of day for a workout.

- **Intensity.** Use descriptive terms or a scale of 1 to 10 (1 is very easy and 10 is extremely difficult). Monitoring intensity levels is a key in avoiding too many back-to-back killer workouts (or in avoiding that crippling disease *couchus potatoeus*).

- **Feelings.** Though many things can affect your mood, a change in mood is sometimes a precursor to sickness and an indication of overtraining. For example, irritability can be an early sign that you're pushing yourself too hard.

- **Injury flags.** Pay close attention to any unusual pain, especially around the joints where most injuries occur. Note any such aches and pains in your log.

- **Weight.** Get on the scale in the morning, after you've relieved yourself. A 3 percent or more loss of body weight might mean you've lost too much fluid. Take an easy day or, better yet, a day off.

- **Weather.** If you are easily affected by heat, cold, humidity, or other weather variables, keep track of these conditions.

- **Notes.** Perhaps the best part about keeping a training log is flipping back to read about that special swim, ride, run, or race.

chapter 3

Getting the Right Stuff

With the plethora of athletic gimmickry available today, it's easy to turn your back on the whole lot.

—Scott Tinley

In a 2000 survey of 925 triathletes conducted by USA Triathlon, 35 percent of triathletes said their bicycles were worth $2,000 to $4,000; another 18 percent valued their two-wheeled steeds at $1,500 to $2,000.

That's not cheap. And, when you factor in running shoes, wetsuits, travel expenses, gym fees, and a couple of trips to the sports massage therapist . . . well, that's a "tri-ing" expense. Where does that leave the average-income triathlete who has to make a decision between buying a wetsuit and paying the rent? Unless you're close friends with Donald Trump, you'll want to get the most from your hard-earned money.

The good news is that you don't necessarily have to spend that much on a bicycle, or any other piece of triathlon gear. The key to being properly equipped for triathlon and not taking out a second mortgage on your house is making smart choices. Part of being smart means not spending a lot of money on a sport that you're only beginning to discover. Put away the credit cards; there's no need to make any rash and expensive purchases without fully exploring your options and understanding what you need versus what you want (or what other triathletes think is cool to have).

This chapter covers the triathlon equipment you'll need for a season full of multisport action, along with estimated cost ranges. We'll take it one sport at a time and cover the basics, as well as some not-so-basic stuff that you might want to consider down the line. You'll find that if you discard the bells and whistles and fancy technology, you won't have to break your budget.

Swimming Stuff

As is the case with much of the equipment we'll discuss, you shouldn't skimp on swimming apparel and accessories. Buy high-quality brands that will last you over the long haul.

Swimsuits

If you don't already own a swimsuit, that's your first order of business. Though a variety of swimsuits are available, you should consider a few issues before purchasing a suit.

First, conventional swimsuits are not designed for bicycle riding or running. As a result, they offer little bicycle padding and running comfort. They are generally very thin and tight, which is fine for lap swimming, but they won't help your sore butt on a thin bike saddle. (It's a personal choice, but in sprint- and Olympic-distance races, most triathletes compete in their swimsuits. There's nothing wrong, however, with donning a pair of bike shorts in the transition area if you prefer. Chapter 10 has more info on transition choices.)

The lack of padding in conventional swimsuits could lead to saddle soreness and the tightness could lead to chafing during the run. In addition, a conventional swimsuit might wear out much sooner or stretch out along the gluteus maximus so that you look like you were last in the port-a-potty line. Look for swimsuits specifically designed for multisports. Some have a thin layer of padding and a narrow design for less chafing along the groin. Some even have a little pocket for your energy bar. You might even opt for a full-blown two-piece tri-race suit, specifically cut and designed for competition.

Second, if you're training with baggy swimming trunks, leave those for water slide time with the kids and get serious with a narrow-style, racing-cut swimsuit. As you'll learn later, it's important to be slippery in the water, and you might be surprised by how much a baggy pair of swim trunks can make you drag in the pool.

Many triathletes own two swimsuits—one for training without padding and another racing suit with some padding for riding and running in shorter- or medium-distance races. (You may have seen those slippery, super-tight high-tech body suits in the Olympics, but those are primarily for competitive pool swimmers and shouldn't be confused for a wetsuit to be used in triathlon open water, since they don't give you the same level of warmth and have no buoyancy benefits.)

The type of swimsuit you choose will vary depending on your preferences and style. Serious male swimmers, of course, tend to opt for the slim-cut or Speedo-style suits, but most men are red-faced about wearing such risqué attire at the local health club or YMCA pool. A good alternative is a men's jammer-style swimsuit, which resembles bicycle shorts, yet fits snugly to give a more modest look without sacrificing hydrodynamics.

To help you get the most out of your swimsuit purchase, make sure to follow the special care instructions supplied with each garment. Most swimwear manufactures recommend that you rinse your swimsuit thoroughly after each use, wash in gentle detergent, and avoid leaving the garment in sunlight. By following these instructions, you'll make your triathlon swimsuit last for at least a season without fading or tearing.

Estimated cost for a triathlon racing swimsuit is $40 for men's and $80 for women's. Tri-race suits range from $75 on the low end to as high as $200 or more on the high end.

Swimming Goggles

Triathletes are divided on the issue of goggles. Some buy the top-of-the-line brand; others just want something to put between their eyes and the water. When choosing how much to spend on goggles, consider whether you will be wearing contact lenses during your swim. If you can't afford to have your vision washed out with the tide, spend some money for a pair of goggles that are durable, resist leaking, and can't be kicked off your face too easily (which is always a possibility in an open-water swim). Know that if you require a prescription lens, your swim budget will significantly increase.

There are many good choices when it comes to swimming goggles—it just depends on how important leaking and comfort are to you. For example, Barracuda swim goggles are form-fitting and come with adjustable and replaceable nose pieces, but tend to be on the pricier side. Classic Swedish-style goggles offer a no-frill design with a flexible fit that retail for under $10. And there is a wide range of goggle brands in between. Finally, you might also consider a goggle with antifog properties and tinted lenses—the greater the visibility, the better your open-water navigation experience will be.

If you can afford to do so, spend the money on a top-of-the-line pair of goggles. When you consider how important goggles are, especially for "water-challenged" triathletes who don't want any surprises on the swim (such as annoying leaks or goggle bands that snap), then spending a little bit more is worth the price.

Estimated cost for swimming goggles: $15 to $50

Wetsuits

A wetsuit offers safety, speed, and warmth to novice open-water swimmers. But do you need one if you just want to finish your first sprint-distance triathlon? Probably not. For longer distances and colder open-water courses, the importance of having a wetsuit increases.

Also, if you're testing the triathlon waters and aren't quite sure you like the sport enough to get good use out of such a purchase, better hold off. Though a wetsuit is an excellent investment for the serious triathlete intent on getting mileage from this neoprene magic, consider buying one only when you have no doubt that you will keep tri ing for many years to come.

Benefits of Wetsuits

The benefits of swimming with a wetsuit depend on various factors, such as percentage of body fat, stroke efficiency, and body temperature. However, there are four areas of consistent return on a wetsuit investment:

1. **Buoyancy.** Wetsuits come in a variety of thicknesses, but all have the advantage of lifting you higher above the water and keeping your body balanced. This advantage is especially helpful to novice swimmers who have poor technique and tend to drag the lower body in the water.

2. **Warmth.** Hypothermia is a constant danger in chilly open waters. Wetsuits keep you warm by trapping a thin layer of water between the fabric and your skin. This layer also keeps you safe and comfortable. (A properly fitted wetsuit ensures that this layer stays intact.)

3. **Energy conservation.** With the increase in buoyancy, you won't have to work as hard to get ahead. That means you shouldn't have to take as many strokes to move through the water. So your stroke count, as well as your energy expenditure, should decrease.

4. **Speed.** Though less-experienced swimmers will benefit more than veterans, wetsuits will help bring that swim time down.

The Wetsuit Cut for You

The wetsuit style or cut that you choose will fall under one of three categories: full-cut, sleeveless, or the most recently introduced short-cut. Your choice should be determined by the environment in which you swim and some personal preferences.

- **Full-cut wetsuits.** Full-cut wetsuits cover your arms and legs and are the warmest and most buoyant. So why look elsewhere? Not so fast. Full-cut wetsuits can be uncomfortable and take longer to get out of, so the benefits might be offset by being slowed in the transition area. In addition, they can significantly change your swim mechanics. Wetsuit manufacturers are continually striving to improve full-cut designs so they are more comfortable and less taxing on transitions. For swims in very cold water, full-cut wetsuits are by far the most appropriate. They are also the most expensive.

- **Sleeveless wetsuits.** Sleeveless wetsuits are the most popular choice for triathletes. For beefy, muscle-bound types, they are the obvious choice. The sleeveless design still provides you with most of the warming benefits but leaves you with complete freedom of movement in the arms, a less harrowing transition, and a slightly smaller bill.

- **Short-cut wetsuits.** In recent years, wetsuit manufacturers have introduced short-cut wetsuits that mimic a design surfers have been using for years. A short-cut wetsuit is sleeveless and extends only to the knees. By sacrificing warmth and buoyancy, you gain time in the transition area with quick exits. In addition, the minimum coverage provides a more natural, less rubber glovelike feel for the swim leg.

SPEED DEMON FACT

Depending on conditions, your technique, and the type of wetsuit you wear, you can shave anywhere from one to five minutes off your time during an Olympic-distance open-water swim (1.5K) with a wetsuit.

Shopping Tips

Are you convinced that you need to get a wetsuit? I'm not surprised. Most newcomers to the sport, especially those who dread open-water swimming, gladly plunk down a couple hundred or so bucks for a little more confidence in the water.

The single greatest consideration when shopping for a wetsuit is fit. The key? Take your time. Until you find a wetsuit that fits you like a second skin, don't be satisfied with anything less. The fit should be tight, but not to the point where you find motion constricted or can't breathe normally. Pay close attention to how the wetsuit fits around the arms (for sleeveless designs) and neck area. These are the two locations where excess water is most likely to enter.

The main fabric in wetsuits is neoprene, a soft rubber that is comfortable, resilient, and a good insulator. However, more and more wetsuits are being introduced with new high-tech materials and specially treated slick surfaces that reduce water drag.

The thickness of wetsuits varies. The smarter designs use a combination of thicknesses and materials within the same wetsuit to facilitate buoyancy and flexibility. For example, many manufacturers use five millimeters of neoprene in the chest and leg areas (for greater buoyancy and a level swimming position) and three millimeters of neoprene or another slick material in the sleeves, neck, and arm holes (for greater flexibility). The thickness you choose should depend on your swimming experience, where you swim (cold or very cold water), and whether you have a tendency to drag.

Of course, cost is certainly a factor. Most full-cut wetsuits surpass the $300 mark and some are as high as $500. Sleeveless wetsuits sell for just under that, and the short-cut designs usually hover around the $200 range.

Estimated cost for a wetsuit: $200 to $500

Bicycle Stuff

If you've only recently been bitten by the triathlon bug, the very first, most obvious symptom is an inexplicable need to visit the nearest bicycle shop. Once you're there, your symptoms might progress toward writing out a check for a thousand bucks, or worse, taking out the plastic. Hold on there. You might not need to shell out four figures at this point.

If you currently own a bicycle and just want to finish your first triathlon, you might be able to get by with what you have until you're sure you'll be a lifelong multisport maniac. It's not uncommon for beginners to use a beat-up old road bike or a fat-tire mountain bike for their first event, and there's nothing wrong with that. However, if you don't have a bicycle (or can't borrow one), then you have no alternative but to look into buying a triathlon bicycle. Also, if you've done a few triathlons and are looking for some advice on making your first serious multisport bicycle purchase, the following sections provide some guidance for you.

Tri-Bikes, Step by Step

Making your entry into the complicated world of cycling equipment can be expensive and intimidating. Somewhere among the fancy designs, shiny components, and black rubber is what you need. Without some basic knowledge, a good understanding of your current needs, and a clear vision of what lurks on your triathlon horizon, there's a strong chance that you'll purchase the wrong bicycle.

Fear not. Here's a step-by-step guide to making that first big multisport purchase, with advice from triathlon bicycle dealers, manufacturers, and coaches. Add to that some tales of woe from professionals who can tell you (through their experience) what *not* to do when you're making that big purchase, and you have no reason to panic.

Step 1: Set a Budget

Walking into a bicycle shop with no plan can mean walking away with no money. Although most bike dealers will not deliberately take advantage of an eager first-time buyer, by setting a budget you are taking the first step toward controlling a situation that might seem uncontrollable.

A cautionary word about overemphasizing equipment is warranted. "Your best bet is buying a reasonably priced, entry-level bike with a clip-on aero bar," says cycling coach Bob Langan. "It all comes to this: It's not the seconds equipment will save you; it's the minutes a good aerodynamic position and proper training will."

How much will you spend on your first triathlon bike? Generally speaking, prices for entry-level racing bikes range from $900 to $1,400. Of course, the sky's the limit on how much you *can* spend (if your bank account can handle it), but spending more than $1,400 is risky for two reasons:

1. You might not know what you need.
2. You might think you know what you need, but you might be wrong.

Does that mean you should go the other way and get the cheapest two-wheeler you see on the dealer floor? No. Although the frugal side of you might want to buy the cheapest Wal-Mart special you can find, you'll likely find it to be less than what you need. Better to buy the most bike you can afford and be able to train and race with comfortably, than have to start all over a few months down the road.

Step 2: Don't Forget Accessories

One common mistake is excluding accessories from the budget. Earmark $300 to $500 for accessories, more if you intend to purchase optional equipment such as an aerodynamic disk, tri-spoke, or deep-rim wheel. Some of the more basic bicycle accessories include the following:

- Frame pump
- Patch kit
- Spare tubes
- Helmet
- Clothing (shorts, jerseys, jacket)
- Gloves

- Cycling shoes (optional)
- Clipless pedals (optional)
- Aerobars (optional, but highly recommended)
- Computer (optional)
- Sunglasses (optional)

As you can imagine, your $900 bicycle purchase can run well into four figures with the addition of these or other accessories. Is all this stuff really necessary? Most of it is. You can't race without a helmet, and you need the additional comfort and safety that cycling shorts, jerseys, gloves, and the other necessities afford you.

If you intend to transport your bicycle in your car, a roof-mounted bicycle rack can run you well over $500. A less expensive alternative is a trunk-mounted rack. Still cheaper is taking the wheels off your bike and throwing it in the back seat or trunk.

You're likely to see some pretty pricey equipment, such as high-end tri-bikes, at your first triathlon. But remember, an entry-level road bike works just fine too.

In recent years, many bicycle manufacturers have included clipless pedals, contraptions that attach your shoes to the bike for an efficient, more comfortable pedal stroke, as basic equipment on entry-level road bike models. This addition will save you close to $150 that you might have earmarked for this accessory. (If the bicycle you're interested in doesn't include clipless pedals, it's time to start negotiating with your dealer.) Though many people fear being attached to a bicycle with clipless pedals, you can get out of the pedals at any time simply by extending your heel outward.

Cycling shoes are designed for use with clipless pedals. Cycling shoes are stiff and transfer energy more directly to the bicycle than do rubber pedals or toe straps. Cycling shoes vary widely in price, from $100 on the low end to more than $200.

Aerobars help you slice through the wind. Better aerodynamics with aerobars increases your speed and helps you save energy for the run. As you train for longer distances, this accessory will definitely fall out of the "optional" category and into the "mandatory" list.

SPEED DEMON FACT

If you recall, Greg Lemond's historic victory in the 1989 Tour de France came as a direct result of the performance advantage of his triathlon aerobars. Wind tunnel testing has shown an estimated average time savings of five minutes during an Olympic-distance bike leg (40K) when a cyclist maintains an aerodynamic position on aerobars. Other studies have shown that cyclists in a proper aerodynamic position are more relaxed and experience decreased heart rates.

Step 3: Understand the Choices and Know What You Need

Purchase a good racing bicycle that is versatile and durable. Buying an entry-level racing bike that is upgradable can save you time and money in the long term. For example, pioneering duathlete Ken Souza's first duathlon bicycle was a Nishiki International he bought in 1982 for a scant $175. Though the bicycle served its initial purpose, it was a touring model (a bicycle designed primarily for casual riding) that Souza quickly outgrew. Yet the pioneering athlete who put duathlons on the map continued to pour money into a pocket full of holes. "It was ironic. I was spending all this money trying to upgrade, trying to save a few dollars by not buying a racing bike. I could have bought a real racing bike sooner if I hadn't tried so hard to upgrade a bike that wasn't worth it." So Souza's experience makes an important distinction—find a good upgradeable bicycle, but just be sure it's something that's worth upgrading over a reasonable period of time, You may very well outgrow an entry-level bicycle, but try and find something that will last you for as long as possible.

Souza's solution to his novice woes was one that you might want to consider if the opportunity arises: "I bought a used racing bike—a Vitus carbon fiber—from ex-pro Mark Montgomery. I think that's one of the smartest things a beginner can do. You'll get top-of-the-line gear, you can get a great deal, and it's usually not beat up."

Again, before you put down any money on a high-tech piece of equipment, ask yourself this: "Just how seriously am I going to take this triathlon stuff, anyway?" Steve Hed, wheel manufacturer and bicycle guru, says, "You have to be honest with yourself. How many hours are you going to spend in the saddle? Are you going to stick with it, or are you going to spend all this money and give it up after one season? Do you want to be competitive, or are you just doing this for fun?"

When you finally look at entry-level racing bikes, you'll find several options available, and several common questions arise. The dealer might bring up these questions, or you might have already begun to ask them:

- **What's the difference between a road bike and a triathlon bike?** Although a bicycle strictly designed for a triathlon is somewhat different from a traditional road racing bicycle, most entry-level road racing models make excellent bicycles for the beginning triathlete. (Later on, you can easily upgrade an entry-level road bike with aerobars, disk wheels or deep-rim wheels, or lightweight replacement parts.) Once you get into the more specialized high-level triathlon bikes, such as those made of carbon fiber and other exotic frame materials, some features such as steeper seat tube angles and 26-inch wheels delineate the triathlon bicycle from the road bicycle.

- **Do I need a special triathlon mountain bike for off-road triathlons?** The short answer is no. If you already own a decent mountain bike that you can comfortably train and race on, then you don't need to visit your local pro shop (other than making sure you have all the accessories mentioned above, nix the aerobars). On the other hand, if you intend to race in XTERRA-type events and own a hybrid bicycle designed for casual road or flat gravel trail riding, then you'll need to muddy up your finances a bit and invest in a fat-tire special that will jump the biggest stumps and get you safely to the transition area without incident.

- **Should I get clinchers or sew-up tires?** This question will likely be irrelevant if your first tri-bike purchase is in the $1,400 range; most entry-level racing bicycles come standard with clinchers, which are wheels with inner tubes and rubber tires that snap into U-shaped rims. Sew-ups are self-contained tires (with no inner tubes) glued onto a flat rim.

  Though sew-ups are the tire of choice for professional racers, clincher tire technology has made it possible to get nearly the same feel, low rolling resistance, and smooth cornering. Unfortunately, many entry-level racing bicycles come standard with low-quality clincher tires that have a high degree of rolling resistance and are puncture-prone. Any reputable dealer will agree to substitute stock tires with a top-of-the-line tire such as a Michelin, Specialized, or Continental without adding more than $80 to the price tag.

- **What's the best frame material: steel, aluminum, carbon, or titanium?** In the past, bicycles made of high-tech frame materials were way out of the $1,400 range. While that's generally still the case, there are some affordable bicycles made of steel, aluminum, and even carbon. Each frame material has subtle, but distinct, characteristics that really come down to riding preference. One camp of cyclists prefers the flexible ride of a shock-absorbing carbon frame, but another camp would rather feel the stiff transfer of power that a steel frame can give. For an even stiffer ride, there's the lightweight advantage of aluminum. Find your preference by taking a few bicycles with different frame materials for a test ride at your local bicycle shop.

It's the Engine, Not the Equipment

Courtesy of Ben Holliss.

There are particular moments in a race that can be especially enjoyable, whether it's finding the perfect draft on the swim or crossing the finish line under your goal time. For Ben Holliss, he finds another typical race moment particularly gleeful.

"In a race, it is great fun to pick off, one by one, these guys on ridiculously expensive aerobikes while I'm riding my beautiful, but basic, road racer," says Ben. "I usually flash a cheeky smile as I pass them by on my no-nonsense bike with basic aero clip-ons and standard race wheels."

Ben is a 23-year triathlete studying for a master's degree in exercise physiology at Loughborough University in the United Kingdom, so he has a unique struggle when he's racing: "Because I work with athletes on a daily basis to improve their performance, this presents a dilemma when I race. I quite often find myself encouraging others during the bike and run, all the while forgetting that I should have my head down and focus on *my* race."

In addition to his academics, Ben is an accomplished cyclist and swimmer with a background in competitive rowing. His achievements include cycling 1,000 miles across England for a charity and cycling 1,000 miles from Barcelona back to the UK. He's also swum the English Channel as part of a four-person relay and plans to attempt a solo crossing soon.

So as gear-oriented as the sport of triathlon can be, which for many tri-geeks is part of the fun, Ben clearly places his priority on substance over style—on the engine over the equipment.

"For me, a really motivating aspect of each race is to dominate those guys with the fancy equipment. I have come to the conclusion that, yes, a time-trial bicycle with an aerohelmet and fancy accessories, like lightweight bottle cages, may save you a few valuable seconds. But it cannot keep you from getting passed by a serious athlete who has put as much effort into training as you've spent upgrading, polishing, and tweaking your wheels."

- **What brand should I choose?** There are many bicycle manufacturers to choose from, and most shops carry several brands. Like an audiophile in a high-quality stereo shop, a triathlete in a good bike shop will find endless options that will do the job and minimal differences between them. In most cases, it will come down to which brand offers you the best value and meets your needs and personal preferences.

- **Should I upgrade the saddle?** Even entry-level triathlon bicycles feature relatively comfortable saddles, but given that triathletes sometimes forgo the thick bike shorts padding during an event, it's important to find a saddle that you can sit with for all those miles on the road. Finding the perfect saddle for your unique rump is a process of elimination—you might have to go through two, three, or more until you find the one that fits just right. Consider upgrading to some of the new anatomically-contoured or gender-specific saddles if you find comfort on your steed to be an issue.

RACING TIP

Prepare yourself for the possibility of a flat during a race the same as you would for a long training ride. Many beginners make the mistake of lightening up the load during a race and forgo the frame pump, spare tubes, and tire levers for the hundredth of a second they might save with less weight. Don't do it. Although some races do have bicycle support that will assist you in changing a flat, most do not.

Step 4: Find a Good Dealer

Where you decide to buy your bicycle is almost as important as the purchase itself. Without advice, service, and accessories to back up your investment, you won't get as much enjoyment out of your new ride.

So do you go with a local bicycle shop or a discount mail firm? Before you take out the credit card and decide to phone in your order for a fast-looking road bike on a catalog page, think again. Though getting a bike through a mail-order company might seem like the wise thing to do, by forgoing a trip to your local bicycle shop, you're cutting yourself off from a wealth of knowledge, information, and personal service.

If you've already decided on a particular brand, there are benefits in going to a shop that has the biggest investment in that line. The salespeople will know more about them and will likely offer you the best deal. If you're not sure who's got the biggest investment, call the manufacturer and ask which local dealer he recommends. The representative you speak to will probably send you to the one he or she knows will do the best job.

Step 5: Buy a Bike That Fits You

Though getting fitted might seem more of an appropriate term when going to the tailor, it's just as important when buying a bicycle. Considering the distance you and your trusty steed will share, a properly fitted bicycle can mean the difference between limping or dashing through a run "leg."

According to John Cobb, a Louisiana dealer who has done extensive wind tunnel tests, fit is very important in relation to performance: "You can take a gifted cyclist and put him on a bike that doesn't fit him, and he'll get beat to death by a much lesser athlete on a good-fitting bike."

The best way to ensure that you are properly fitted on your bicycle is to find a dealer willing to spend some time with you and look at your position on the bike. By setting up your bicycle on an indoor trainer and taking a few measurements, a knowledgeable dealer can make a big difference in how comfortable and efficient you are in the saddle. From the height of the saddle, to the fore and aft position of your body, to the height of your handlebar stem, all these factors and much more will affect your fit and help you feel like you and your bicycle are one.

Step 6: Use Your Investment

There are probably as many newly purchased entry-level racing bikes gathering dust in garages as there are wedding dresses tucked away in attics. Take the time to learn about bicycle maintenance and get involved in group rides, two pragmatic ways that will be as essential to your triathlon success as making a wise initial investment.

Proper maintenance of your bike is vital, too. First on your list of things to learn should be how to change a flat. Have someone you know show you how, or ask your bicycle dealer. Though gearing and your derailleur might seem intimidating, learn some simple techniques to help keep your components clean and in sound working condition. Your dealer might offer maintenance workshops and classes. I'll provide more information on maintenance in chapter 5.

Estimated cost of an entry-level triathlon bicycle: $900 to $1,400

Choosing a Bike for Off-Road Triathlons

A growing trend in triathlon is the concept of an off-road or mountain biking cycling leg, as evidenced by the popularity of the XTERRA events. These and other similarly muddy events put a new wrinkle on the traditional road cycling makeup of a triathlon. They also potentially introduce the sport to a whole new audience—mountain bikers.

If you aren't familiar with mountain biking and would like to participate in an off-road triathlon, such as an XTERRA triathlon, you'll need to hang up your sleek triathlon bike with the skinny tires and go fat.

Your approach to choosing a steed for an off-road triathlon should be identical to selecting a good mountain bike. As with all bicycles, consider proper fit, your budget, and necessary accessories. Here are some tips:

- Stay away from hybrid bicycles. They typically don't have the durability and wheel traction necessary for true off-roading.
- Make sure you add a good pair of handlebar ends for better leveraging when climbing. Most off-road races really challenge you with daunting climbs.

- If you're comfortable with them and have the extra money, clipless pedals are a good accessory, giving you more power and control on climbs.
- Don't forget a bike pump and a place to store your extra tubes and tire-changing tools—your road bike frame pump probably won't fit your off-road ride.

Running Stuff

Although certainly not as pricey a sport as cycling, running can get expensive if you let it. Between the latest high-tech jackets, running shorts, socks, and shoes, well, you could be looking at several hundred dollars. Is there any need to spend that much in preparing for your triathlon adventure? Again, probably not. Your old, worn-out windbreaker and the high-school gym shorts with the holes in them will do just fine for now. But there is one piece of running equipment you definitely don't want to skimp on: shoes.

About 20 years ago, I hobbled into a medical tent with blood blisters on two of my toes after completing my first marathon. Being the inexperienced runner that I was, I had done the Chicago Marathon in running shoes that didn't fit quite right. In hindsight, I don't think the shoes I ran in during that first 26.2-miler were too large or too small for me. They just weren't the right shoes for my feet.

If you come from a running background, you've probably found a good shoe that works for you. Once you've found a running shoe that provides just the right amount of cushioning, support, stability, and comfort, keep buying 'em. It's not a bad idea to buy several pairs and stock up because shoe manufacturers regularly discontinue models. (If you are new to running, you'll find some practical advice on choosing the right shoe in chapter 6.)

Regardless of your running background, if you haven't found the perfect shoe, find a local running specialty shop as fast as your feet will take you there. As with cycling, you will greatly benefit by picking the brains of people who have specialized knowledge. The personnel at a running store can guide you in purchasing the right shoes for your feet. Most times, you'll find friendly, knowledgeable people who are runners themselves and like nothing better than to turn you on to the right shoe.

Of course, you'll save money by going through mail-order catalogs or to a large sporting goods chain. But if you don't know exactly what shoe is best for your foot, running style, and the goal you've set, then buying a running shoe without the guidance of a runner at a local specialty shop is taking a shot in the dark.

Many specialty shops are also much more willing than sporting good chains to let you take a test drive, either on an in-store treadmill or around the block. It's important to do because you need to feel how your foot fits the shoe as you run. Although the shoe might feel great whil you're walking around, running is the best way to tell if the shoe is right for you.

Be prepared when you visit your local running shoe store. The more information you can provide to the salesperson about your running and goals, the better he or she can match you to the right pair of shoes. Here are a few things you should talk about:

- Distance covered per week
- Type of surface you usually run on (asphalt, grass, trails, gravel)
- Type of running injuries you've experienced in the past

Estimated cost for running shoes: $75 to $150

Calculating Your Total Triathlon Equipment Costs

Now that you have a general idea of how much this triathlon stuff will deplete your savings account, let's do some addition. Fill out the Equipment Cost Worksheet. You might already have some of this gear. If not, perhaps borrowing or buying used is an alternative for you.

Equipment Cost Worksheet

Item	Estimated cost	What you can afford
Racing swimsuit	$40-$80	
Swimming goggles	$15-$50	
Wetsuit	$200-$500	
Bicycle	$900-$1,400	
Bicycle accessories	$300-$500	
Running shoes	$75-$150	
Other:		
Other:		
Total:		

From J. Mora, 2009, *Triathlon 101*, 2nd ed. (Champaign, IL: Human Kinetics).

PART II

Triathlon Training Basics

Not every newcomer to triathlon comes from a swimming, cycling, and running background. You might have some experience in one or two activities or perhaps no real competitive experience in any of the three. The following part applies to a varied group of triathletes, from the experienced endurance athlete to the aspiring weekend warrior. Each chapter contains a Dos and Don'ts section for those with little or no experience in each leg of the triathlon, but even you veteran swimmers, cyclists, or runners can find some of the training tips and workout schedules helpful.

chapter 4

Swim Training:
The Key Is Technique

One doesn't discover new lands without losing sight of the shore from time to time.

—André Gide

More than two decades ago, I found myself in a beginners' swim class at Daley College on the south side of Chicago. It was the middle of winter, and I was learning the front crawl in the hopes of completing a triathlon the following summer. I was starting from square one.

I was 23 years old, and I couldn't go one lap in a pool without gasping for air. I had a fear of water, especially deep water; this fear had been with me all my life. When I was 10 years old, I nearly drowned in a hotel pool. That left an indelible imprint on me and contributed to my general ineptitude and anxiety in the pool.

But my ego and childhood fears aside, taking a swimming class was the right move to make. Little by little, drill by drill, I graduated from walking across the pool mimicking the front crawl stroke to actually stroking and sticking my head in the water at the same time. Later, I added the kick, and voila! I could swim a lap. Within a few months, I was swimming. I signed up for intermediate swimming and then advanced swimming with Coach Hajak, who helped me hone my skills for open water.

By the time triathlon season rolled around, I was a swimmer, albeit a slow one. I was the last out of the small lake in Bloomington, Illinois, at my first triathlon in 1989. (My open-water navigational skills were not quite up to par—I zigzagged a lot.)

My swim training was the most challenging aspect of training for my first triathlon, and I'll always consider learning to swim one of my greatest personal achievements. Not just because my learning to swim enabled me to finish my first triathlon, but because I managed to look in the eye a personal demon that had stared me down for 13 years.

The Water-Challenged

Take an informal survey of most triathletes, and I'm sure you'll find that my story is not unique. Although the fears, lessons learned, and experiences are different, many triathletes find swimming to be the most challenging event. In some ways, that's ironic. First, the swim usually takes up the least time; cycling and running make up the majority of a race. Second, swimming is generally less taxing on the body than cycling and running, particularly forgiving to leg muscles and knee joints. Third, unless open-water conditions are unfavorable, the energy expended during a swim does not typically match that of the bike ride and the run (except for pros and other top age-group athletes competing for prize money or accolades).

So with all the good news about swimming, why is it such a big deal, especially to many first-time triathletes? There are probably as many answers to that question as there are triathletes. For whatever reason, learning to swim and training properly might be your biggest obstacles to reaching your triathlon goal.

RACING TIP

Sometimes learning to relax about swimming is a matter of attitude. Many triathletes look at the swim leg of a race as simply a warm-up to the hard part—the bike ride and run. You might find that hard to believe, but when you graduate to longer distances, you'll find that to be true. Even if you're doing a sprint-distance race, try thinking of the swim leg as a warm-up. Then maybe that quick dip won't seem so intimidating.

If You're New to Swimming: Dos and Don'ts

If you're just getting your feet wet in swimming, don't be intimidated. All it takes to learn how to swim is a little courage, self-discipline, and some good instruction. As with the next few training chapters, I'll provide some dos and don'ts for the first-timer:

- **Do take a beginners' swim class.** Do like I and many other triathletes have done—seek instruction at a local city college or adult-education course. The YMCA in your area might also offer swim classes. If you look hard enough, you'll find a beginners' class to get you started on many happy laps.

- **Don't recruit a friend as an instructor.** Don't make the common mistake of recruiting someone you know that you *think* might be a good swimmer (or who might *say* they are a good swimmer). Oftentimes, those reputations or self-concepts are inflated, and rarely will you get good instruction this way. Your best bet, again, is to seek professional instruction from a swim coach who conducts a class.

- **Do stick with it.** As discussed in a bit, swimming is more technical and skill oriented than cycling and running. Therefore, learning to swim the front crawl properly involves learning a sequence of skills. These skills are often taught independently and then combined gradually. Exhaling underwater, turning your head to breathe, stroking, kicking, maintaining good body position—acquiring these and other skills is a methodical and painstaking process. Be patient and have faith in your instructor. Though the prescribed drills might seem mundane and wear on you mentally, practice them in the order they are given. You'll be glad you did later on.

- **Don't jump the gun.** There's nothing worse than feeling discouraged. A sure way to discourage yourself from learning to swim is to attempt a full-blown lap swimming workout when you've only taken one week of instruction. Again, swimming is a technical sport, and it takes time to perfect technique. Practice the drills, and worry about lap swimming later.

- **Do practice on your own.** A better way to use your energy than trying to lap swim too early is to set aside some time away from class to practice the drills learned in your last class. When I took beginners' swimming, I knew I wouldn't be ready in six months for my first triathlon if I just attended the twice-a-week classes without some extra effort. So I set aside three additional days during the week when the pool was open for practicing the drills I'd learned the previous class.

  Also, when you are first learning a new activity, it's best to get in as much practice as close to the instruction as possible. That way you learn faster and retain more. If you're serious about learning to swim, set aside at least two or three sessions per week—even if they are 15-minute sessions—for practicing the most recent lesson on your own.

- **Don't learn bad habits.** Although you might feel at a disadvantage if you are new to swimming, you are learning to swim the front crawl properly. Because technique plays a big role in swimming, bad habits abound. Just sit in on a masters group swim session at a local YMCA. You'll see arms flailing and slapping the water in every direction, horrendous flutter kicks that send spouts to the ceiling, and bad breathing habits that make you wonder whether there are enough lifeguards on deck. By being a newcomer, you can avoid bad habits that will slow you down with every meter you swim. Even if you aren't completely new to the front crawl, concentrate on letting go of any bad habits you have developed by learning technique via drills all over again.

If You're Already a Swimmer

If you're entering the sport of triathlon from a swimming background, you have a significant psychological advantage over many triathletes who dread the swim leg. Here are some tips you should keep in mind if you've got gills instead of lungs:

- **Focus on technique.** Even veteran swimmers need to continually hone their efficiency in the water. If you've developed bad habits, such as a lazy stroke in one arm or a flutter kick that churns up water, now's the time to improve in those areas. Remember, you've got to bike and run after a swim, so the more efficient you are, the better off you'll be.

- **Learn open-water skills.** This tip goes for everyone, but if your swim background comes primarily from pool swimming, then you need to experience open water. Dealing with waves and navigating a race course are skills that pool swimming doesn't teach you. (More on open-water swimming later in this chapter.)

- **Become a land lover.** Don't spend all your training time in the pool. Swimming makes up the shortest portion of a triathlon. Spend the majority of your training time cycling and running.

TYPES OF SWIM TRAINING

You can integrate many types of workouts into your schedule, each fulfilling a unique and specific objective. You should base your mix of swim workouts on your current swimming capabilities. For example, if you're still learning to swim the front crawl properly, then focus on technique drills. The possibilities of what you can do in the pool are endless, but here are general descriptions of three main types of swim workouts.

- **Interval training.** These are sets of moderate- to high-intensity short swim laps, with a short, timed rest in between. In most sports, interval training is a key component to developing aerobic capacity and increasing stamina. In swimming, it can also help your technique.

- **Set distance or timed swims.** These can be a set number of laps without stopping or a predetermined time close to what you might experience during a race. This is mainly to build stamina; however, it's important that you use proper technique throughout.

- **Drills.** For the beginning swimmer, drills should make up a good chunk of your swimming time. Each drill focuses on a specific aspect of proper swim technique.

Going to Camp

Terry Laughlin is an expert swim coach and founder of Total Immersion Swim Camps. He is also an author and has put on swim clinics around the world. If you've been around triathlon for a while, there's no missing the Total Immersion way of swimming. Much of what I and countless other triathletes have learned about proper swim technique has come from Terry, either though the numerous articles he's authored for every major triathlon magazine, his DVDs, books, or the swim camps he puts on throughout the nation.

I first attended his swim camp several years ago, going into the camp with a long-held misconception about swimming. Having a fairly trim and lanky build, I assumed that my lack of buoyancy put me at a natural disadvantage in swimming. I reasoned that, sure, I'd be able to compete in triathlons (with the aid of a wetsuit), but I would never be very fast in the water. As a result, I divided almost all my training time between running and cycling and hoped that backpack propeller motors would be sanctioned for racing.

With my running and cycling speeds peaking and my race times still unsatisfying, I decided to tackle the swimming issue head on and was fortunate enough to spot an ad in *Triathlete* for Total Immersion Adult Swim Camps. "You should be able to shave minutes off your 1.5 kilometer time after the three-day camp," Terry said when I requested an application over the phone. I was hopeful, but nonetheless skeptical. He told me that the camp focused on technique as opposed to conditioning, drills instead of workouts. Though I'd been a consistent practitioner of drills, I felt that my lack of buoyancy should be offset by developing upper body strength and stroke power.

"After this weekend, you'll realize that good swimming is not about buoyancy or body fat or upper body strength. It's about getting your body in the right position," said Laughlin during the orientation. "It's about balance." At the camp, I learned key principles of swim training that have helped me swim more efficiently, faster, and with less effort. The camp was a mix of classroom instruction and pool time, but we spent a large portion of the weekend drilling, and drilling, and drilling.

The first key principle Laughlin introduced us to was swimming balance. Using a partner on the pool deck, we did an exercise that showed us the proper balance position for swimming. The point, Laughlin stressed to us, was that with proper balance and keeping the head connected to the rest of the body, you'll stay horizontal in the water (as opposed to the familiar sagging lower body that I had accepted like unwanted baggage).

After some instruction on a pool drill to help establish balance, and with my partner watching me, I jumped into the pool to test the theory. To my amazement, my buttocks skimmed the surface of the water as I did a relaxed kick. I could feel it instantly. The experience was similar for most of the other participants, some showing obvious shock in their ability to stay horizontal in the water. "I thought that there was no hope for me," said triathlete Greg Jay Valent. "For the last two years, I've felt more tired while swimming, and I was getting slower, like I was fighting the water. I can already tell this will really help me."

"The biggest impact you can make in swimming is not by increasing your power," said Laughlin. "It's by eliminating resistance through balancing. In the water, you're moving against something that's a thousand times more dense than air, so a horizontal position and staying balanced throughout each phase of the swimming stroke is crucial."

Toward the second half of camp, the second key principle Laughlin demonstrated was hip rotation and "swimming on your side." Through a series of classroom instructions and pool drills, the concept that greater arm extension and power came from rotating the hips was engraved in our minds. "The engine is not in the arms and shoulder; it's in the hips," said Laughlin. "If you look at the top swimmers, they don't have huge upper bodies. They don't power through the water. Great swimmers stay balanced and rotate their hips so that they use the least amount of energy necessary to accomplish the most."

By the second day of camp, many other triathletes and I began to accept that interval workouts and long swims were not the keys to better swimming. Schooled in "the more mileage, the better" mentality, I began to realize that swimming required an altogether different approach. "You have to look at swimming as a motor skill activity, like tennis, golf, or skiing," said Laughlin. "And look at conditioning as something that occurs as a result of practicing technique. Triathletes

Focusing on drills and proper technique during training will soon have you exiting the swim with plenty of energy to spare!

tend to have difficulty seeing this because most come from a running or cycling background."

Laughlin's swim drills are too lengthy to go into here in great detail. Besides, you'd learn them better from him than from a single chapter in a book (visit his Total Immersion Web site at www.totalimmersion.net). But I did ask Terry to address the specific swim training information the beginner or newcomer to the sport needs to succeed. Toward the end of this chapter, he also briefly describes a few fundamental drills. So for now, I'm stepping aside to let Terry Laughlin, the master teacher, do what he does best: teach swimming.

Terry's Shrewd Tips for Your First Triathlon Swim

Nothing against the hundreds of experienced triathletes I've coached in Total Immersion workshops, but I've got news for everyone who might be thinking of tackling a triathlon. If you work the swim right, this sport is only two-thirds as tough as you think it is. Although there's no question that endurance counts—name another sport that calls a two-hour race a "sprint"—the process of training for a triathlon needn't swallow you whole. You just need to know how to minimize the work that does you the least good.

Two Good Reasons to Relax

You'd never find the word *relax* in the gospel according to most triathletes, which says you simply train and train until you can keep moving for anywhere from 2 hours (sprint) to 16 hours (Ironman). Training usually means just one thing: mile upon mile (or kilometer upon kilometer) of swimming, running, and cycling.

At first glance that strategy might make sense, but looked at more critically, there's strong evidence to suggest that time-consuming endurance training is far less helpful for swimming—and may even hurt your performance—than it is for biking and running. If I'm right, you can cut distance off the weekly training volume you thought you'd need for a creditable swim leg.

Reason one is that the swim comes first in a triathlon. In a sprint triathlon, most competitors are finished with the waterborne quarter-mile or half-mile in 20 minutes or less. But you might not be dismounting your bike until 90 or more tough minutes have ticked by, and a lot of new triathletes will still be out there on the running course two hours or more after they started their day's labors. When is a serious energy shortage most likely to develop? Right, later in the race. So cumulative fatigue—and the need to train yourself to resist it—is obviously much greater in running and biking than in swimming. On top of that, think of the limited work your swimming muscles do compared to your cycling and running muscles. The swim leg is always the shortest of the three, typically lasting just one-third to one-quarter as long as the run and bike legs.

The second reason to cut back on your swimming training time is that swimming, compared to running and biking, is fundamentally an unnatural activity in which practice—without coaching, at least—does not make perfect. In running or cycling, where mechanical efficiency is so much higher, more training distance makes a positive difference; in the water, it's a waste of time and energy for most people. When you swim more and more distance, as you do in most tri-training programs, you're more likely to be practicing your mistakes than refining your technique and boosting your endurance. You're not becoming a more efficient swimmer; you're just getting better at swimming inefficiently.

Efficiency is what triathlon swimming is all about. It's not how fast you finish the wet leg, it's how easily. You've got a lot of work ahead of you once you're back on land, and saving energy might be the most important thing you can do in the water to help your overall finishing time. Standing behind the starting line on race day, think of what you're about to do in the water after the gun goes off as simply a way of getting to the real race start, the bike. Triathlon swimming and triathlon swim training should be more about race management than about racing. So train like a manager, not like a machine. It's not how strong you are; it's how you use your strength.

Escaping the Planet

From his marathon USTA league tennis matches that always seem to go three sets, to long workouts at the gym with his basketball pals, to his endless laps in the pool, Joseph Picciuca is the epitome of athleticism. While this impressive exercise regimen may only seem like the design of a fitness nut, it is much more than that to Joe.

"I love working out, playing tennis, and swimming and playing basketball," he says. "It helps me forget the Planet and all my problems."

The "Planet" Joe refers to is his job, a maintenance worker at "Planet" Wal-Mart. And, although he proudly holds a master's degree in history and bachelor's degree in journalism, Joe currently finds himself limited in his career options, which is something he hopes to change. That's because Joe has Asperger's syndrome, a mild form of autism that affects many areas of his life, including social interaction.

But as with many unique challenges in Joe's life, he's looked to athletics as a way to both escape and cope. That's why he's chosen to expand his athletic resume and train for his first triathlon, which he hopes to achieve within a year.

"I want to do a triathlon to prove to myself that I have the discipline to swim, bike, and run," the 36-year-old says. "Plus I want to feel the rush of competing in a long-distance endurance event with other people and spectators cheering me on."

Joe is well on his way to competing in his first triathlon and dedicates a large portion of his training to swimming, his weakness, which he's determined to turn into a strength. (He wisely plans to compete in an indoor triathlon for his first, since the pool swim may be less intimidating.) Between his tennis matches and basketball scrimmages, he runs regularly on the track. And he integrates cycling workouts by running errands on his bicycle on the streets of Crest Hill, Illinois, where he lives in an apartment complex.

"Finishing my first triathlon would make me really happy. I know I can do it because I'm working really hard, especially in the pool."

Terry's Fish School: Intelligent Triathlon Swim Training

Fish go farther and faster on less energy than we'll ever manage. But we can borrow some of their most efficient techniques by using the nervous system, not the cardiorespiratory system. This Total Immersion plan replaces simple distance, repeats, and intervals with strategies for fishlike swimming:

- **Count your strokes regularly.** Your best measure of efficiency is how many strokes you take getting from one end of the pool to the other. As fatigue mounts and efficiency falls, your stroke count can balloon by 30 percent or more as you diligently train your nervous system to lapse into inefficiency.

- **Practice stroke elimination.** Make efficiency, not distance or speed, your objective. Set a stroke-count target of 10 percent lower than your norm. For example, if you usually take 22 strokes per length on endurance swims or repeats, set a new limit for yourself of just 20. See how far into a swim or set you can hold that count instead of how fast you can finish or how tight an interval you can manage. (Note: You should swim easier, not harder, on your lowest count; don't strain to bring it down.)

- **Streamline yourself with skills.** Whenever you're not counting strokes, work on getting your nervous system accustomed to efficiency-promoting skills that make you more fishlike. None of these skills comes naturally, and all take work to get used to, but they produce results. These three skills will make an immediate difference:

  1. **Hang your head.** Head–spine alignment is essential to efficient swimming.
     In practice: Release your head's weight to find its most natural position; never hold it up. Look directly down, not forward.
     In the race: Let your rivals do all the work of looking; just follow the swimmers ahead of you, limiting your peeks forward to once every 20 strokes.

  2. **Lengthen your body.** A longer body line reduces drag, allowing you to swim faster, easier.
     In practice: Focus on using your arms to lengthen your body line rather than pushing water back. Slip your hand and forearm into the water as if sliding it into a mail slot.
     In the race: Don't barge through waves or chop; instead try to slice through them.

  3. **Move like water.** Water rewards fluent movement and penalizes rough or rushed movement.
     In practice: Pierce the water; slip through the smallest possible hole. Swim as quietly as possible.
     In the race: During the race, make it your goal to be the quiet center of any pack you're in, stroking slower and with less splash than all the flailing arms around you.

- **Swim less, drill more.** If, despite your best efforts, you find yourself unable to reduce your stroke count to a consistent 20 strokes per 25 yards (about 23 m), you're better off doing more drills and less swimming. Your stroke inefficiencies are so stubborn that every lap you do makes them more permanent. The only way to break those bad human swimming habits and build new fishlike ones is to spend more time doing drills than conventional swimming. Try doing at least 60 percent of your distance in stroke drills for the next month or two and see how your stroke reacts. Even when you do reduce your stroke count to 20 strokes per 25 yards, drills should constitute at least 25 percent of your total workout time. Happy laps!

Terry's Tips on Overcoming the Open-Water Willies

For many triathletes, it's not swimming that is feared, it is swimming in open water. Whether in a small lake, one of the Great Lakes, or the ocean, open-water swimming can make first-time triathletes extremely anxious.

For Those Who Fear Taking the Plunge

Carol Zanoni turned up at one of my Total Immersion swim camps hoping to fulfill a dream. The Teaneck, New Jersey, athlete runs a strong marathon and can bike like a seasoned racer, too, but her first attempt at a triathlon ended in disappointment when she suffered a panic attack just a short distance into the swim leg and had to drop out. Her goal: learn to swim comfortably and competently in open water and make it to the bike leg.

How many other thousands of would-be triathletes, people who can run all day long and have perfectly good bikes in the garage, still shrink from their first race? It's that open-water swim. Even those who may be able to cruise, gracefully or otherwise, from one end of the pool to the other recognize that swimming without a line to guide you, a bottom you can see, and a wall nearby for comfort is a whole other story. Buoys to find, surf (and other competitors) to fight, and who knows what else is in the water out there. Who needs it?

Then there are those who aren't afraid of open water; they just can't swim very well in it. I can't count the number of triathletes who showed up at one of my camps this year saying, "Just once I'd like to come up to the beach and see some other bikes besides mine in the transition area."

I've offered both types the same advice. Although your success in the bike ride or run is primarily a measure of how well you've trained, success in the swim leg depends mainly on how well you've practiced. Adopt a new philosophy for the pool: Conditioning is something that happens to you while you're practicing technique and pacing skills.

If you can swim for 30 minutes nonstop in the pool without feeling wiped out, there's no reason you can't handle the open-water swim leg of a triathlon without too much hassle. Success in the swim leg involves two steps: intelligent preparation in the pool and strategic rehearsal in open water. Neither one's a workout; both are practice.

Practice in the Pool

There are many ways to prepare for open-water swimming in a pool. In my swim camps, I teach various drills and activities, each designed to achieve an objective that can help you swim better in open water. It's impossible for me to teach these lessons to you here. But at the least know that you can learn tangible techniques to make open water much less nerve-racking.

These drills and activities include the following:

- Stroke drills provide greater stroke efficiency through practice of the three streamlining skills described on page 58.
- Sensory swimming focuses on one specific sensation (such as feeling balanced).
- Stroke eliminator swims test your stroke efficiency.
- Longer swims use greater stroke efficiency for consistency.

Practice in Open Water

Before the race, do some swimming in a lake or the ocean. It'll get you used to the absence of convenient guides like lane lines. You'll learn to navigate using on-shore landmarks. For safety's sake, swim with an experienced partner or a group, or with a canoe or kayak escort, or in water you know very well. In cold water, stay close to shore. Hypothermia (lowered body temperature) can compromise your coordination and judgment. Wear a wetsuit if the water makes you feel very chilled.

Don't just swim; practice the same technical points you've been practicing in the pool. The idea is to smoothly transition from your pool practice to an open-water race, so make it an open-water practice. Swim downhill, reach forward with a weightless arm, roll your hips from side to side, and so on. You can't count laps out there? No problem. Count strokes instead. Practice a technique for 100 strokes or more. Not having walls actually makes it easier. Your rhythm isn't interrupted, and you'll find it's easier to groove your stroke.

Some Fundamental Swim Drills

Here are the first few swim drills that I teach in my Total Immersion workshops. My drills are designed to teach skills in progression, with one drill laying the foundation for the next. Thus these few drills provide only a glimpse of the fundamentals needed for "fishlike" swimming.

Superman Glide

This drill teaches you to cooperate with gravity, as you sink into a horizontal position. In shallow water, push off the wall or bottom and glide forward without kicking. Extend your arms at shoulder width and hang your head between your shoulders. If your legs start to sink, just let them. Stand and catch your breath when you lose momentum. Repeat several times, trying to travel a bit farther each time. Your goal is to experience a few moments of weightlessness and effortless travel, no matter how brief.

Superman Flutter

When you can't extend your Superman glide farther, add a flutter kick—but with a difference. You'll focus more on streamlining your legs than kicking them. Start from Superman glide, as described previously, with a focus on getting your legs to draft behind your torso. If they begin to sink or if your momentum slows, begin to kick gently. Kick just enough to keep your legs from sinking or to maintain a lazy glide. Stand whenever you need to catch your breath. Repeat several times, trying to make your kick a bit more relaxed, streamlined, and quiet each time.

Start Swimming

Start where you left off previously. Push off into Superman glide, but this time, begin stroking as your glide slows, aiming mainly to feel that the weightless sensation has reduced your need to kick. Take only three to five strokes—or stop as soon as you feel the need to kick again. Catch your breath, then repeat. Each time, try to increase your sense of *allowing* your legs to respond to body motion—a passive kick. Keep swimming so long as you feel it. Stop as soon as you don't. And make your strokes as quiet as you can. When you have a new sense of balance and ease, try a full length or two. Compare your effort and stroke count to your pre-drill swimming.

Laser Lead Flutter

Start from Superman glide (SG), but pull both arms back as you begin kicking. Continue in this position until you need a breath. As you practice, focus on releasing your head until you feel the water support it. Then focus on your laser beam—an imaginary projection of your head-to-spine line. It should always point where you're going.

Raise your laser to feel how balance is affected. Then release your head and feel easy balance return. This is the same head position you will use in all subsequent drills and whole stroke. Your final focal point is to feel as if you're being towed by a line at your head, which lengthens the line between your head and toes. Speed is unimportant. Instead, focus on minimizing drag so a light, compact, and quiet kick moves you forward.

Core Balance: Rotate Just Enough

Push off into SG. Glide a moment, then begin kicking. Pull your arms back, drop a shoulder toward your chin, and keep your head stable. Rotate just enough for your shoulder to clear the surface. Maintain this position, kicking gently, until you need a breath. As you practice, focus on rotating just enough for your shoulder to clear the surface. You will likely find it difficult to hold this slightly rotated position.

You'll need to use core muscles to remain stable at that degree of rotation. This is the same rotation you will use in all subsequent drills and whole stroke.

Skating Position

Push off into SG and progress to core balance position as previously. When you feel stable, sneak the lower arm forward, following a track in front of that shoulder. Avoid having your hand move in front of your nose. While kicking gently, focus on the following details, one at time. Don't progress to a new focal point until the one you are working on begins to register in your muscle memory.

- Hang your head so your laser points forward.
- Keep your extended arm slightly outside shoulder line. Check the following: Hand is relaxed. Fingers are down. Wrist is slightly below elbow.
- Rotate just enough to clear one shoulder.
- Align your body. Be spearlike.

As you practice, imagine a target at your fingertips on the lead arm. Your hand should spear to this exact position in every freestyle stroke from here on.

Dynamic Skating

Push off into SG. As you begin kicking, pull one arm back while extending the other forward, rotating as you do. Your goal is to hit the target mentioned earlier with the extending arm. Once in skating, recheck the focal points listed earlier. Repeat this 6 to 10 times, alternating the arm you pull back. Each time, your goal is to move easily from the prone Superman glide position to the slightly rotated skating position.

SG to Skate to Swim

Begin exactly as previously, but after glide kicking easily for a moment in the skating position, begin stroking. At first, take only four to six strokes before standing for a breather. During those strokes, check one of these focal points. Segue to other focal points after the first registers in your muscle memory.

- Laser beam points forward and your head's weight is supported by the water.
- Hand extends on the shoulder-width track.
- Fingers spear through your imaginary target.
- Body, from torso to toes, is aligned behind your lead arm.

Material attributed to Terry Laughlin is used with the kind permission of Mr. Laughlin. www.totalimmersion.net

chapter 5

Bike Training: Putting in the Mileage

A focused training program that combines fitness, technique, and mental preparation will produce peak performance.

—Lance Armstrong

It's often said that triathlons all come down to the run. I disagree. Although you certainly have to be a good runner to be competitive in triathlon, you first have to come off the bike with legs that haven't been mangled beyond their running abilities.

A good example of this is my rivalry with my friend, Guillermo. In my early days of triathlon racing, Guillermo was a much better runner than I was. From 5K road races to marathons, the longer the race, the farther I finished behind Guillermo. When we entered the world of multi-sport, I took to cycling with as much enthusiasm and energy as I had done with marathoning. Guillermo, on the other hand, avoided putting in distance on the bike. He was nervous about riding on roads, even low-traffic ones, and never quite got the hang of dealing with the close proximity of other cyclists in group rides.

As a result, I became a better cyclist, although I could run no faster. Because we were of equal swimming ability, I assumed that our cycling and running times would offset each other, and that we'd finish any triathlon at about the same time. Much to my surprise, I was maintaining my lead off the bike and consistently crossing the finish line well ahead of him. What had changed? My run times were about average, if not slower than usual, so I knew I wasn't running any faster.

In reviewing the race results, I saw that Guillermo had slowed on the run because the cycling had beaten him up so much. Without the proper training and necessary cycling distance under his belt, he would start the run on sore, tired legs, sometimes coming close to cramping. It didn't matter that he had a better runner's body than I, or that his marathon best beat mine by more than 30 minutes. By not properly training on the bike, he had effectively negated his natural running ability.

The lesson to learn is this: Although most triathlons finish with a run, it doesn't matter how good a runner you are if you don't have legs left off the bike. So what if you're not interested in competing, but just hoping to finish your first triathlon? The same lesson applies.

Cycling: The Core of Triathlon

Because many triathletes come from a running background, cycling is often the second most feared event of the three. Although cycling is usually not as intimidating as open-water swimming to the newcomer, there are many reasons some triathletes avoid two-wheel training. Some find the speeds too nerve-racking, or perhaps the danger of riding in traffic is a factor. Others simply find cycling uncomfortable or monotonous.

No matter what your aversion is to cycling (if you have one), understand this: Riding comprises the majority of time in a triathlon. No matter how you train, you'll spend most of your race on a bicycle saddle. So if you're not used to the idea of doing some riding, now is a good time to get used to it.

That's not to say you will necessarily find bike training to be unpleasant. You might find the open roads to be an escape from everyday stress, group rides to be great social outings, and the dizzying speeds of downhills to be peak experiences.

If You're New to Cycling: Dos and Don'ts

Although almost everybody has done some recreational cycling, organized or competitive riding might be new to you. The rules of the road are still the same (although many recreational cyclists don't follow them), but the penalty for breaking them can be a severe accident. Here are some dos and don'ts for those of you who haven't ridden your Schwinn since you were knee-high:

- **Do ride with traffic.** Cycling on the road is an exhilarating experience, but it's vital for you to follow the rules of the road if you want to stay safe and injury-free, especially if you're limited in your training course by high-traffic roads. Contrary to daredevil bicycle messengers you might see in busy downtown streets, the proper (and legal) way to ride on roadways is with traffic, not against. Another common error is weaving in between parked cars, which makes it difficult for motorists to see you until it's too late. Ride in a straight line, avoid erratic or sudden turns, and ride defensively.

- **Don't ride on busy streets or paths.** It amazes me when I see serious cyclists riding on busy roadways, with hundreds of cars whizzing by them within inches of their limbs. Not everybody has the good fortune to live near rural roads; living in large cities makes it doubly difficult to find open roads for cycling. But thousands of bicyclists are hit, sometimes fatally, by cars on highly trafficked roadways. If you don't live near rural roadways with low traffic, get yourself a bike rack and drive to a location that has safer training routes. Yes, it's a pain and takes more time from your busy schedule, but your ride will be much more enjoyable and, best of all, safer. Another tip: Try to ride during times when there might be less traffic on the roadways.

- **Do participate in group and organized rides.** Bicycle clubs and shops in virtually every well-populated area of the country sponsor weekly rides, and longer organized rides take place almost every weekend. Organized rides are an ideal way to train, providing you with an opportunity to mix with a group of men and women who are near your current riding ability. Most large groups consist of a wide range of riding talent, from the slowpoke talkers to the stone-faced quad machines. Weekend rides with frequent food stops range from 20 to 100 miles (32 to 161 km); they are excellent opportunities to get in a good chunk of mileage without having to worry about carrying enough fluids and food with you. These events also help with the mental obstacle—the boredom that can set in when riding distances over 25 miles (40 km).

- **Don't ride an uncomfortable bike.** I've talked about how important it is to get a properly fitted bicycle, but I can't stress this point enough. Nobody likes to be uncomfortable in an activity that might last an hour or longer, and riding a bicycle that doesn't fit or is uncomfortable is just no fun. Other factors that affect comfort are the choice of a bicycle saddle (no real rule of thumb here—you just have to keep trying them until you find one that fits your unique butt) and padded bicycle shorts.

- **Do be ready for anything.** Unlike swimming in a pool at the YMCA or running within a few miles from your doorstep, cycling can take you some formidable distances. You might find yourself 10 or more miles from home, perhaps on some country road without a soul in sight. So it's important to be ready for any mishap, mechanical or otherwise, that might occur.

First and foremost, never ride without a bicycle helmet. Be sure you know how to fix a flat; have a friend or someone at your local bicycle shop show you. Carry at least two tubes and a pump (or CO_2 air cartridges) with you at all times. Even if you're not mechanically inclined, carry a multipurpose cycling tool that will fit in a behind-the-saddle frame bag for simple repairs.

Always carry a credit card, driver's license, and cash. For longer rides on rural roads, a cellular phone and some extra snacks and water are a good idea.

- **Don't be intimidated.** Newcomers to the sport might find cycling intimidating for a couple of reasons. First, the expensive tri-bicycles you're sure to find in the transition area of any competitive triathlon (particularly hotly contested, large events such as Ironman qualifying races) are enough to make anybody rolling in with a mountain bike or old clunker feel ashamed. Don't be. As discussed in chapter 3, there's no need to spend a ton of money on bicycle stuff at the onset, especially if you're just beginning in the sport and aren't interested in competing. Roll in that clunky, but trusty, steed of yours in the transition area with pride!

  Second, if you happen to begin to ride with road racers, not triathletes, who are dedicated solely and seriously to cycling, you might find their approach a little more intense. As you'll find in chapter 7, triathlon training and training in individual sports are two very different approaches. Don't be alarmed or put off from cycling because of your exposure to "roadies." No matter what type of competitive cycling (criteria, time trials, road races, track racing) these serious cyclists are training for, their methods of training will be different.

CYCLING ETIQUETTE

As a newcomer to the sport of cycling, you might not be familiar with some basic cycling etiquette and jargon, which can really bite you in the saddle at your next group ride. When riding in a group of riders, communication is key. For example, when passing another cyclist (always on the left side) be sure to shout a warning: "On your left." Or, when you turn a corner together, you might hear "hold your line," which is your fellow roadie's stern reminder that you should be sure to turn cleanly and in unison with the rider in front of you to avoid erratic turns and the potential for an ugly multi-wheel accident.

There are many other rules of the road when it comes to cycling that might seem strange to you at first, but each serves a purpose. The best strategy in learning and adapting to road riding in a group is to be upfront and honest about your newcomer status, asking the leader about any specific etiquette or rules that you should know. In fact, doing so can help establish trust and respect among your newfound roadie friends . . . at least until they leave you in the dust.

If You're Already a Cyclist

Just as a veteran swimmer has a psychological edge over those who dread water, a seasoned cyclist entering multisports has a *physical* advantage over anybody with little cycling experience. Here are some things to keep in mind if your quads have their own zip code:

- **Get used to riding alone.** If you come from a road racing background, then you might be quite good at drafting and comfortably riding in a paceline. (More on drafting later for those not familiar with the term.) However, triathlons are more like time trials than road races, so adjust your training accordingly. You can still do the occasional pro bike shop ride or road race for fun and competition, but make sure you do the majority of your training without drafting.

- **Get over any aversion to aerobars.** It took the road racing community a long time to accept aerobars, and some traditionalists still scoff at their use, even for time trialing (although they are now in the minority). Aerobars provide a significant performance advantage, and my guess is that, as a veteran cyclist, you want to do well on the bike leg of a race. Aerobars will help you do that (more on aerodynamics and aerobars later in this chapter).

- **Get in the pool and pound the pavement.** The temptation might be to focus on becoming a better cyclist, but your efforts are better spent focusing on your weaknesses, not your strength. Cycling will comprise the majority of time in any proper triathlon training program, but that doesn't give you license to skip the other two sports. One tip: Many cyclists love the sport because of the camaraderie it affords. If this is the case for you, join master swimming groups and running groups to help motivate you for those activities.

Spinning Your Way to Success

Even if you can't quote the gear ratios on your bicycle (I can't either), you're probably somewhat familiar with your bike's multiple gears. These gears allow you to change resistance to accommodate your current ability level and the varying terrain. You're no doubt aware that some gears are very easy to pedal, and others send your quadriceps into overload.

Learning to use gearing to accommodate workout goals and handle varying terrain effectively is a skill that you gradually acquire by experimentation and practice. Little by little, you'll learn which gear you feel most comfortable in—the one that doesn't feel too hard or too easy for the moment. Your inclination might be to find the biggest possible gear to mash. Until your legs (particularly your knees) adapt to the cycling motion and you are confident that your cycling ability has reached a competitive level where speedwork becomes a viable training technique, however, hammering big gears will do you more harm than good. You'll cause undue and potentially damaging stress and strain on your knees. And you might find yourself overtrained and burned out.

What exactly is spinning? Spinning is pedaling at high RPM (revolutions per minute) to increase efficiency. More importantly for the beginner, spinning is a safe way to avoid knee injury, learn correct pedaling technique, and adapt to the unique motion of cycling. Most experts contend that pedaling at 85 to 95 RPM is a good spinning range. How do you know your RPM? The best way is to purchase a computer with a cadence feature, which displays your RPM at the push of a button. Without a computer with cadence, it's difficult to tell if you are spinning, especially for a novice cyclist.

In general, the resistance when you are spinning should feel relatively easy, but not so soft and rapid that your pedaling motion becomes choppy, erratic, or out of control. Pedaling should feel smooth, and your focus should be on completing the entire 360-degree pedal stroke efficiently, without any "dead spots" or bursts of power. Each pedal stroke should feel controlled and tight all the way around. If you train in a hilly area, it's more difficult to spin throughout an entire workout. Use your entire range of gears, and don't be afraid to use your easiest gear (largest cog and your smallest chain ring) to maintain high RPM on uphills.

Although we'll go into specific training workouts and recommendations in chapter 7, it's important to note that spinning should make up the first few hundred miles of cycling. In fact, for shorter or middle-distance triathlons, spinning might be your entire training method.

Please note: In recent years, mainstream fitness enthusiast have embraced "spinning" classes that somewhat mimic the training described here. However, this type of indoor training on a stationary bicycle adds other elements and isn't spinning as described here, in the strictest sense. Group indoor "spinning" classes are fun and can augment your training down the road, but don't neglect a base of easy and high-revolution road riding before you start pushing bigger gears or increasing resistance, whether indoors or out.

The Drafting Thing

Unlike the swim leg of a triathlon where you'll often be an arm's length away from a fellow competitor, cycling rules prohibit close proximity to other riders. Why is that? Simply put, the triathlon is designed to be based on individual effort, and sometimes riding close to another cyclist provides a teamwork and performance advantage called drafting.

Drafting means riding in another cyclist's slipstream, which makes it easier to cut through the wind. Although drafting usually occurs when a rider rides closely behind another cyclist, you can also draft by riding behind and to either side of a cyclist. (This is why USA Triathlon prohibits amateur triathletes from riding within a range that covers the entire circumference of another rider.)

To understand why drafting is not allowed, you need to understand the significant performance advantage it allows. The best way to do that is to try drafting with a training partner. When you are heading into a strong headwind on an open, straight stretch of road, ride behind your friend's rear wheel. Instruct your friend not to make any sudden turns or brake (unless in an emergency).

If this is your first time drafting, don't get too close. One foot is fine. Although experienced road racers who thrive on drafting get within an inch or less of another rider's wheel, it's best to stay at a relatively safe distance. Don't get in your aero bar position. Place your hands on your brake hoods or on your brake levers, just in case. Keep your vision focused on what's ahead on the road so you will always be aware of any forthcoming hazards.

You will feel an immediate difference; wind resistance will drop dramatically. Considering that wind is your primary foe on the bike, drafting is a big deal. Depending on the direction of the wind and the proximity and location of your wheel to the lead cyclist, your effort level can decrease by anywhere from 10 to 40 percent while you are maintaining or even increasing your speed.

Drafting and Racing

Obviously, drafting goes against the basic principle of competing in triathlons, which is to test individual endurance. For this reason, drafting is not allowed. However, you might have heard of certain drafting-sanctioned races. This fairly new development is strictly limited to the professionals competing in races put on by the world governing body of triathlon, called the International Triathlon Union (ITU). The thinking is that drafting-sanctioned races are more exciting to watch. Thus the ITU has pushed the rule change to garner more publicity and Olympic inclusion.

And while most triathlon purists consider such events a stain on the sport, it's not likely you'll ever participate in a triathlon that allows drafting. Even the ITU doesn't allow drafting-legal cycling legs for age-group triathletes.

But in the event that you do participate in a draft-legal race, it's vital that you get experienced with road training in a peloton (cycling pack). The best way to do this is to visit your local bicycle shop or contact a cycling club in your area for group rides.

> ### *RACING TIP*
>
> If you do enough racing, sooner or later you might be victimized by a fellow competitor who has decided to take the easy way out and ride your wheel. Although you might not be voluntarily aiding this person, USA Triathlon officials can disqualify all riders in a drafting situation, regardless of who is drafting whom. To avoid this penalty, be aware of other competitors around you. If somebody tries drafting you, tell him or her to back off. If that doesn't work, pull off to the side and let the little weasel face the wind without your help.

While at first riding in a group with your tires inches away from other riders might seem intimidating and more than a bit scary, you'll find that over time, you'll learn to relax and enjoy the rush and whirl of a speeding peloton down an open road.

Drafting as a Training Tool

Most triathletes choose not to draft during training rides because the best way to train for time-trial cycling is to become accustomed to the aero position and solo riding without the aid of a slipstream. However, in certain situations, drafting can be useful. For example, during group rides where packs form or a pace-line is organized (a pace-line is a line of cyclists taking turns breaking the wind on a rotating basis), participation depends on drafting. There's nothing wrong with training this way, providing it doesn't comprise the majority of your riding.

Also, when riding with a training partner of superior riding ability, drafting can help you stay with him or her and put in more distance than you might be able to do by yourself. Your partner should agree and know that you are drafting, so he or she doesn't turn or brake suddenly.

Lastly, when done with a dependable partner, drafting can help you concentrate on your pedaling form and efficiency. With the wind at bay, spinning in a slipstream can help you focus on completing a full-circle pedaling motion. One note: Unless it's otherwise agreed on, drafting etiquette dictates that riders take brief turns breaking the wind. To put it more eloquently, don't "suck wheel" without "breaking a little wind" yourself.

Training Technique Basics

The kind of cycling you'll be doing for triathlons, known as time trialing, primarily requires endurance. Although cycling is not as technical as swimming, there are some important technical considerations for the beginner or newcomer to the sport.

Learn Bike-Handling Skills

If you frequent pro cycling shops or hang around USCF (United States Cycling Federation) bicycle racers, you might find that triathletes get a bad rap. In some ways, it's undeserved. After all, triathletes have been responsible for many cycling innovations that have brought new life into the sport: aerobars, aerodynamic wheels, super lightweight cranksets, stems, and other replacement parts have all come about or been popularized as a direct result of triathlon. Heck, they should be glad we came along.

Yet, in one respect, we triathletes deserve a little ribbing from our cycling brethren—we just aren't as good at handling our bikes. Time trialing (riding all by yourself from point A to point B) requires very little bike-handling skill. If you can pedal, make a turn, and hit your brakes, you can complete a ride. But just because good bike-handling skills aren't a necessity doesn't mean you should avoid learning them. The ability to handle your bicycle in a variety of situations, some of them emergencies, can save your life or, at the very least, prevent a serious case of "road rash." Also, these skills will give you a sense of mastery of your bicycle, giving you more confidence to train effectively.

Many fundamental bike-handling skills will come naturally when you start putting in some distance. Another good way to learn these skills is to ride with more experienced cyclists and do what they do. If you don't know any experienced riders, seek instruction from your local cycling shop. Some of the most important skills to learn for safe cycling are cornering, braking, emergency braking, and hill climbing, which I will cover in more detail later in the chapter.

Getting Aero

When the "safety bicycle" was invented in 1885 by English bicycle manufacturer J.K. Starley, little thought went into aerodynamics. The focus then was on creating a functional frame for two wheels of equal diameter. Most conventional bicycle frames today are a derivative of the old-fashioned diamond geometry invented over 110 years ago.

Fortunately, today we know a lot more about aerodynamics. Even if you intend to finish your first triathlon cycling leg in an upright position on your granddaddy's bomber, you might want to know how important aerodynamics are, just in case you decide to give this triathlon stuff a more serious go.

Aerodynamics 101

To understand the importance of the aero bar and good aerodynamics, let's take a look at the four basic ways air moves around you on a bicycle:

- Air moves over the top of your head.
- Air moves around your right side.
- Air moves around your left side.
- Air moves around the bicycle frame, between your legs, and under and behind you.

In three out of these four categories, you can help yourself slip through the air better. Three things can reduce the drag caused by air traveling over your top and around your sides:

- A proper aero position
- An aerodynamic helmet
- Aerobars

Find the Aero Fit

Another good way to find your ideal aero position is to have the good people at your local specialty bike or triathlon shop take a look at you on your bike. They can help you make the proper seat, stem, and handlebar adjustments to improve your comfort level and aerodynamics. Often these bike fittings involve taking a number of exacting measurements (for example, your position relative to the stem, crankarm, and other "landmarks" on your bike), because even minor changes can help alleviate stress on your arms or give you greater pedaling extension power.

For example, it's important to adjust your seat height so that the knee is very slightly bent near the 6 o'clock pedaling position. You'll know your seat is too high if it causes your hips to swivel at the 6 o'clock position of the pedal stroke. Swiveling hips can lead to soreness or, worse, a lower-back injury. On the other hand, if

your seat is too low, your knees will bear the brunt of all that downward pressure, which might send you scurrying to the sports doc. Also, a seat that's too far forward or too far back can make your knees sore, as well as your neck, shoulders, and back. See diagram at left for an example of good road-riding position. As shown, elbows should be kept slightly bent. Note that using triathlon aerobars will change your position so that your back is more flat, making your entire stance much more aerodynamic for a relaxed and efficient ride.

Bike-Handling Safety Tips

Maybe you're not used to the speeds of a bicycle with thin tires or riding on the road. Bike-handling skills are even more important when you ride in a group. And learning to be comfortable and safe on your bicycle means practicing safety skills, such as emergency braking, hill climbing, and turning corners. It's best to find an experienced rider to teach you these core skills, but here are a few quick tips to get you started.

- **Emergency braking.** When you have to abruptly stop, brake your rear tire first and hardest, using your front brakes as additional, but secondary, braking power. And, if time allows, shifts your weight backward, pushing your arm and upper body straight out so that your bottom sticks out behind the saddle. A lot of this is split-second timing, but it's a crucial—potentially life-saving—skill you can learn and practice on a rural road, away from traffic and other riders.

- **Hill climbing.** When climbing a steep hill, be sure to pace yourself, brace your hands on the top of your brake hoods for leverage, and gently rock back and forth as you peddle up and down. If you abruptly come to a stop before hitting the peak, simply click out of your pedals (if using clipless pedals) and catch yourself.

- **Downhill riding.** Flowing down a downhill curving road at dizzying speeds can be a peak experience, but, until you've mastered it, be sure to slow to a comfortable speed as you ride downhill. Also, pay special attention to potholes, obstacles, traffic, and other hazards.

- **Cornering.** Turning at high speeds is similar to downhill riding—reduce your speed until you are comfortable doing it. Be sure to lean slightly into the corner and position the pedal on the corner side up to avoid it hitting the pavement as you turn. Focus on making a clean turn, something that will come in handy when those roadies tell you to "hold your line."

Camera 4/Imago/Icon SMI

Practicing clean turns in training will help reduce your chances of causing a nasty pileup on race day.

Handling the Roads

Courtesy of Marti Greer.

Although there are plenty of unnerving things about getting into competitive cycling, such as high-speed downhills or riding in a pack, Marti Greer's biggest fear was pedals. After her winter purchase of an entry-level racing bike with clipless pedals, Marti realized she didn't feel comfortable attaching her feet to anything she couldn't simply lift her foot off of whenever she needed. Veteran cyclists know that clipless pedals are virtually as easy to exit as conventional ones, requiring a simple twisting motion to detach oneself. Nevertheless, Marti needed to feel comfortable with the concept, so she set up her bike on an indoor wind trainer and practiced attaching and detaching herself from the clipless pedals.

"When I finally started riding outside in the spring," says the 50-year-old resident of Birmingham, Alabama, "I felt OK being attached to the pedals. It might sound silly, but I needed to feel comfortable with it before I got on the roads. It also took me awhile to learn bike-handling skills, which I'm still doing."

Marti's triathlon friends guided her through some of the major handling skills she needed in order to stay vertical on the bike. They taught her to shift body weight into a fast turn, position her pedals at the 12 o'clock position on the cornering side, and put her hands in just the right place on the handlebars. "I'm still getting used to riding," says Marti, who completed her first triathlon, a sprint-distance race, in early 1997. "Now I'm more confident and more relaxed on the bike, which really makes training and racing a lot more fun."

To date, Marti has complete 178 triathlons, including four Ironman-distance finishes. She now counts cycling as one of her strongest disciplines and has added weight training to help her develop more power and prevent injury.

Types of Cycling Training

As with running, there is a wide variety of cycling workouts to choose from. Chapter 7 covers workout planning, but the following is an overview of some typical workouts. If you are a beginner, some of these workouts, such as long rides, road races, and hill or power workouts, are not advisable until you get more experienced.

- **Building block rides.** These very short rides increase endurance and accustom the beginner to extended time on the saddle. Do them at a relatively easy pace, preferably spinning. These rides should start at 5 miles (8 km) and gradually increase to 10 to 15 miles (16 to 24 km). Saddle soreness is a very common symptom—don't worry; the muscles in your buttocks will harden, and the pain will eventually go away.

- **Medium-distance rides.** These rides are most useful for those training for an Olympic-distance race (40K cycling leg). They can range from 20 to 30 miles (32 to 48 km), and the intensity depends on the race goal.

- **Long rides.** These rides are typically performed at a slow, even, conversational pace. They can range from 40 to over 100 miles (64 to 160 km). The goal with long rides is primarily to increase endurance.

- **Recovery workouts.** These workouts are short rides at a low intensity, with a lot of spinning. They can range from 5 to 20 miles (8 to 32 km). The goal in these workouts is to recover from a difficult or long workout. Spinning during recovery workouts helps to loosen up legs and alleviate soreness or fatigue.

- **Time trials.** Do these race simulation rides on a course with few or no stops and at an intensity that is close to or at your desired race pace. They are typically half of what the actual race distance is.

- **Group rides.** The intensity of these rides depends on the group. Most group rides go 25 to 40 miles (40 to 64 km). These rides can be killer workouts, great social gatherings, or a bit of both.

- **Road races.** Many road races are USCF-sanctioned and therefore require a membership license. However, some races have a Citizens category for non-USCF members. You can participate in USCF 40K individual time trials, which are ideal race simulation workouts. Or you can try a road race, which can range from 20 to over 50 miles (32 to 80 km), but road races will test your bike-handling skills, so don't attempt them until you are confident you can ride in a pack.

- **Hill or power workouts.** If you are fortunate (or unfortunate) enough to have some hilly terrain where you live, hill climbing can help you increase your strength and power, which are two components that will help you go faster. If not, you can accomplish similar results with power workouts, which integrate sprinting intervals in the middle of a ride. One warning: These workouts are considered speedwork, and you should not attempt them without first completing the base training discussed in chapter 7.

- **Off-road training.** If you are training for an XTERRA-type race or similar event that includes a mountain biking leg, take to the single track for your training. Find the most challenging trail nearby and visit it often on your mountain bike. Trail riding is much more technically difficult than road riding. You have to become comfortable with jumping stumps, dealing with slippery surfaces, and climbing wicked hills; otherwise you'll find your race experience to be a muddy nightmare.

Cycling Advice From a Pro

When professional triathlete and coach Lauren Jensen races on the circuit, you can immediately tell her apart from the others by the rubber shark attached to the top of her bike helmet.

"I started wearing the shark helmet at the '91 Ironman Triathlon Championship in Hawaii," says Lauren. "I wore it because I wanted to remind myself that the most important thing for me on that day was to have fun. I've worn it at every race since then."

Having "Jaws" riding with her isn't Lauren's only claim to fame. Since she turned professional in 1993, Lauren has won over 50 triathlons. Lauren considers cycling to be her strength. Because she is a longtime coach to many beginning triathletes (including her mom), and author of several magazine articles about triathlon, I've asked her to provide some guidance and tips for your triathlon bike training and racing.

WHY DO MALE TRIATHLETES SHAVE THEIR LEGS?

This is perhaps one of the most frequently asked questions from newcomers to the sport. Competitive cyclists have been shaving their legs for many years, primarily because it reduces the vulnerability to infection from road rash, which is a scraping away of a layer of skin from a fall off the bike (a fairly common occurrence among pack-riding cyclists). Hairless legs also make care and treatment of road rash easier and less painful.

Triathletes shave for the same reason, although road rash is not as common due to the less hazardous nature of time trialing. There are other reasons male triathletes choose to shed their leg hair:

- It's easier to massage your legs or have a therapist work on them without hair.
- You can get in and out of a wetsuit faster.
- It's easier for your body to be marked with your race number before a triathlon.
- You might find that it helps keep the legs cooler during a hot run.
- You can show off your fabulous triathlete legs.

The "Shark" on Taking a Bite out of Fear

In coaching triathletes new to the sport, I typically find an element of fear in their thinking. It's normal to have some fear of the unknown, and for many of us, a triathlon can present a whole bag of unknowns. Those who fear speed, accidents, or mechanical breakdown may think of the cycling leg of a triathlon as particularly scary.

Others fear dropping out, finishing last, or looking foolish. Unfortunately, this fear is what keeps many from attempting a triathlon. However, those who do make it to the starting line find that once the gun goes off, triathlons are not as overwhelming as they thought.

The right cycling training should help alleviate many of your fears of not finishing. As for finishing last, the odds are against it. But even if you do finish last, you are ahead of everyone who didn't even "tri." Triathlon training is a learning experience, and you'll gain confidence with each race. After racing for over two decades, I am still constantly learning things that make my racing faster and more enjoyable.

Lauren's Cycling Tips

I have several suggestions to help your cycling training and racing be more successful. Some of these ideas might be common sense to you, yet all of these tips come from mistakes I have made or have seen others make.

- **Use your gears wisely.** Don't push a gear that's too hard and wears down your legs (remember, you've got a run to do). Keep your cadence up around 90 RPM. Anticipate what gear you will need to be in for any hills and shift early so you don't have to grind up the hill.

- **Practice using new equipment.** Don't enter a race with new bike parts that you haven't tested and mastered beforehand. This applies to aerobars, clipless pedals, saddles, wheels—just about anything on your bike that could adversely affect your riding. This advice is especially important for clipless pedals; make sure you can stop and dismount safely before using them in a race.

- **Practice U-turns.** Why a U-turn? Many races with out-and-back bike courses have a U-turn turnaround where you have to navigate around an orange cone. Many triathletes, even experienced ones, have found themselves kissing the road at these turnarounds. Find a safe place to practice sharp corners and U-turns that you might find on a race course. As in a race, always take them slowly.

- **Hydrate on the bike.** Many beginners wait until the run to start drinking fluids. That's a big mistake. You should be on a full tank of gas as you start the run, so don't forget to drink on the bike.

- **Wear a helmet.** Helmets are required during races, but don't skip wearing one during your training. A helmet saved my life once. Even veteran cyclists can crash through no fault of their own. Don't be foolish and assume that you'll be safe without a helmet.

- **Keep your bike in good shape.** The two most common mistakes novice cyclists make are not keeping their bike chain lubricated and not keeping tires at the proper pressure. Both can results in mechanical breakdowns, such as a broken chain or a flat tire. Buy lubricating oil and ask your bike shop owner about its proper usage. While you're there, buy a floor pump with a built-in pressure gauge.

- **Take a lighthearted approach.** I have a rubber fin on my bike helmet to remind me what triathlon is all about: fun. If you need to be reminded of this when your training and racing get too serious, you can find rubber sharks in the toy department.

6

Run Training: Putting One Foot in Front of the Other

Running, or some other form of exercise, is essential in the drive to become and perpetuate the ultimate self.

—George Sheehan

South of Phoenix is a small tribe of native Mexican Indians with amazing running skills. This tribe is called the Tarahumaras. From birth to death, they run and run and run without pain or discomfort. They are known to chase down deer and horses and run anywhere from 40 to 150 miles (64 to 240 km) in one day! Locals there often tell a joke that attests to the extraordinary running skills of the Tarahumaras: A tourist who was driving by a running Tarahumara stopped and asked if he would like a lift. The Tarahumara replied, "No, thanks. I'm in a hurry."

A group of researchers asked a group of Tarahumaras to run 26.2 miles to test their heart rates and blood pressure. (The Tarahumaras agreed, but found it amusing that they would want them to run *only* 26.2 miles.) The results were unbelievable: Pulse rates averaged about 130 beats per minute, and blood pressure readings, which were low at the start, were even lower at the end of the staged marathon (Connor 1978).

So what does this tell us about running and triathlon? First, it demonstrates that the potential for running performance and endurance is much greater than scientists are willing to admit and that most of us (except these native Mexicans) can imagine. Second, it suggests that the Tarahumaras are an example of the potential of triathlon. After all, they usually don't run just once a day; they perform a variety of daily activities, transitioning into running as the need arises. Most of all, the Tarahumaras are a shining example of the potential within all of us to achieve what we might have previously thought unachievable.

Having Something Left

Whether you come from a running background or are new to the sport, the last leg of a triathlon can be the most demanding, both physically and mentally. You or I might not have the running gifts of the Tarahumaras, but certain training techniques and workouts will help you avoid a death march at the end of a race.

Perhaps the best way to avoid the tired triathlon shuffle is not a running training technique at all, but proper pacing through the swim and the bike ride. Setting a maniacal pace through the swim and the bike ride is a common mistake of the first-time triathlete, especially one who has attained a certain degree of competency (and arrogance) with swimming and biking (keep this in mind during your next triathlon race).

Proper race pacing aside, training for a good triathlon run leg means following many of the same principles veteran runners have followed for years. If you're a runner making inroads into multisports, that doesn't mean that your triathlon run schedule for a sprint-distance race should be identical to your 5K training. Like anything in life, it's not that simple. There are a few twists and turns and some new ways of training, and you might need to sacrifice mileage for other activities—swimming and biking, for example.

Admittedly, of the three activities that comprise triathlon, multisport running bears the closest resemblance to its individual sport sibling. The main differences are not so much about running itself, but how it fits into the bigger picture of triathlon.

If You're New to Running: Dos and Don'ts

As with all sports, there is a right way and a wrong way to do things in running. Unfortunately, many non-runners just beginning multisports lack knowledge of the basics and, as a result, run themselves into a brick wall. If you're new to running, one of the first things you need to do is learn the fundamentals, from equipment to training to safety concerns. So let's look at some beginners' dos and don'ts:

- **Do run in good running shoes.** It may sound *too* basic, but you've probably seen it before, most often at the health clubs: Novice runners wearing basketball high-tops circling the one-hundredth-of-a-mile indoor running track. (Which is another mistake: Never run on a track smaller than your bedroom because you'll put a lot of stress on your body, in particular ankles and knees.)

Become an educated consumer. First, accept that you need a running shoe—your tennis or aerobics shoe is not designed for the high-impact and stable rear foot control that you need. Then find out what kind of running shoe is best for you. Read *Runner's World* or *Running Times* magazines for shoe reviews, and visit specialty shops that specialize in running. (There's more on selecting the right running shoes later in the chapter and in chapter 3.)

- **Don't run with headphones.** For music lovers, combining the experience of running to Mozart's "Eine kleine Nachtmusik" or Coldplay's "Speed of Sound" heightens the enjoyment, but for safety reasons, pounding the pavement with your favorite tunes blaring in your ear is not a good idea. Although listening to headphones is fine for treadmill running at home or in the health club, you won't hear approaching traffic, cyclists, dogs, and other hazards on the road.

- **Do wear comfortable running clothes.** Wear something breathable. The human body has a built-in air conditioning system called sweating. Help your body do the job it was designed for by wearing light shorts, singlets (sleeveless T-shirts), and socks designed to wick sweat away from your body. The wetter your feet, the more likely you'll experience friction-related injuries such as blisters and black toes. And wear light-colored running clothing that doesn't absorb heat.

- **Don't be afraid to walk.** If you've never run before, the best way to begin is to run for a few minutes at a time, and then walk, and then run again as your current fitness allows. Everybody starts out this way, so there's no reason to feel ashamed about it. Even experienced runners training for a marathon intersperse walking breaks during long runs to help their legs recover.

- **Do follow the rules of the road.** Like drivers and cyclists, runners have their own rules of the road. Novices often disobey these rules at the expense of their own safety. The best possible scenario is to avoid running near or around traffic. But when you are forced to hit the roadways, use common sense—run against traffic, not with it. The reason is simple. When you run with traffic, you can't see what's going on behind you. If a car is weaving all over the road behind you, you have no chance to react.

- **Don't run in dark, isolated areas.** Crime is something we don't like to think about when we run, but the reality is that you have to take precautions. We've all heard the horror stories, and instead of becoming one of them, it's best to stick to running routes that don't put you in jeopardy. After the sun goes down, stay away from secluded parks or trails that might prove dangerous, especially if you live in a high-crime area. Not to sound paranoid, but criminals use the cover of dark and seclusion to set their traps, and you don't want to be the mouse. So run in well-lit, populated areas. If you can't avoid a dark stretch or secluded area, at least have your wits about you and try to anticipate any possible "surprises."

If You're Already a Runner

Of all three sports, the run leg of a triathlon is the one most apt to catch off guard the novice who hasn't trained properly. If you're a veteran runner, believe it or not, you might be in for the same surprise unless you do more than just pound the pavement. Here are some tips for the seasoned harrier:

- **Dive in the pool and pedal down those roads.** Those runner's legs might churn like a steam engine during that Sunday morning 10K, but if you don't balance your training, your legs might feel like rubber after a hard swim and bike ride. Although training in the other two sports will likely cut into your running time, the more balanced approach of multisport training can rejuvenate your road-weary legs.
- **Don't fret about distance covered.** Many serious runners count the miles they run as though they were balancing their checkbooks. Know that your weekly distance will likely decrease as you add swimming and cycling to your time equation. Don't sweat it. Remember, the goal is balanced training.
- **Follow hard runs with easy bike rides or a swim.** If you're a performance-oriented runner doing hard workouts such as intervals and hills (more on this later), you've probably been following those intense sessions with an easy run the next day. After planning your triathlon training, if you decide to keep doing these tough run workouts, make sure you don't follow them up with a hard bike workout. Apply the same hard/easy principle to multisport training and go for a relatively short and easy ride, or better yet, a swim.

Watching Your Step

By far, most injuries that occur to triathletes are running injuries. Although there are several reasons for this, the simplest explanation is that running is stressful on the body. Every time you put in a hard run, you overstress your muscles. On a physiological level, you are tearing cell membranes. It sounds pretty scientific, but all it really means is that pounding the pavement puts a pretty good wallop on your legs.

Through the years, runners have found that interspersing running with rest has helped to avoid injury and improve performance. As the popularity of multisports grew, cross-training became an additional tool for helping the body to recover, as well as a way of staying fit without running all the time. Inevitably, even the most dedicated runner cross-trains to spice things up, which also explains why most triathletes come from a running background. Sometimes the issue is forced by the all-too-common running injury. Sometimes the motivation is performance; you can gain only so much improvement by putting in more or faster distance.

Most running injuries result from inadequate rest and recovery time. Planning and following a smart and effective training schedule that builds in rest days and easy training days for recovery is crucial to avoiding injury. The problem is that many runners are bundles of nervous energy when it comes to rest. Running can become an addiction, albeit a healthy one. Without the soothing effect of the runner's high, many harriers find themselves out of their element when they take an extended period away from running.

Fortunately for us triathletes, training in more than one activity significantly improves our chances of staying healthy. Cross-training distributes the stress of running over the entire muscle network. No one muscle group is likely to be taxed beyond its limits. For example, marathon runners are particularly susceptible to overuse injuries because of the constant stress and strain of using the same leg muscles.

More than likely, the distance you are training for is in the 5K to 10K range. Although you might not be putting in the distance of a marathoner, these hints will help you train safely and effectively:

- **Build a solid foundation (base).** We'll get more into base training in the next chapter, but it's worth mentioning here that base training is a particularly important component of run training. Running requires muscle strength and involves high cardiovascular and respiratory demands, so it's vital that you progress gradually, taking steps along the way to let your body recover.

- **Follow time, not distance covered.** It's far easier to track your running progress using time, not distance, as your measuring stick. Don't worry about measuring your running routes, or whether you've put in enough distance for your race (which is always a topic of debate, anyway). Just set your sports watch on the countdown timer mode for the desired time of your run. If you have an out-and-back course, set your watch to beep at the halfway point. Tracking time is also much less distracting than counting miles or kilometers and often helps to avoid excessive distance that can lead to overtraining or injury. The sample programs you'll find in this book follow this rule to help simplify your training.

- **Follow the 10 percent rule.** Experts contend that you shouldn't increase your weekly distance by more than 10 percent. For example, if you've run three times this week for 20 minutes each workout for a total of 60 minutes, next week's running time should not exceed more than 66 minutes. The week after that, you can increase your running time to 73 minutes (10 percent of 66 rounded to the nearest digit is 7 additional minutes).

  The second thing to remember about this rule is that you should *back off* by 10 percent every third or fourth week of training, depending on how well you recover and the length of running time we're talking about. That means you should decrease your running time for one week, and then continue increasing your time again by 10 percent, beginning where you left off. This decrease gives your body a bit of a chance to catch its breath from the increases in training and the cumulative stress you've put your legs through for three or four weeks.

  If any of this confuses you, or you're not good with numbers, don't sweat it. The main thing you need to remember is to increase your distance gradually and put in an easier week of running workouts once every month or so.

- **Plan your workouts accordingly.** Plan your harder running workouts for days that aren't too close to other hard workouts. For example, if you do a hard cycling ride on Wednesday that leaves your legs feeling like spaghetti, Thursday would not be a good day to put in a long run. Allow yourself an easy day both before and after hard runs. If you don't, you're risking injury.

- **Go for consistency.** The most frequent mistake new runners make when training is going out too hard and then blowing up after the first few minutes. For every run, make your goal consistency so that your body adapts to prolonged hard efforts (like in a race). You don't teach your body and your mind good pacing by having erratic running workouts that, if you charted the pace, would look like the stock market. Try to maintain an even pace throughout your runs.

- **Concentrate on your form.** Form isn't as crucial in running as in swimming or even cycling, yet good form does make a difference in avoiding injury. Focusing on form teaches your body to hone in on biomechanical improvements and to run more efficiently. Don't dwell on it too much, especially if you're a beginner. Just concentrate on running relaxed, smoothly, and naturally, without any unusually jarring foot strikes. Everybody has a different running style; try to get a sense for yours, while focusing on possible improvements that might reduce unnecessary stress on knees, hips, and even the upper body muscles. See the diagram and quick tips below to help you find your form.

1. Minimize excessive bouncing motion.
2. Relax your upper body, especially the shoulders.
3. Find the stride length and cadence (number of steps you take to cover a distance) that you feel comfortable with.
4. Keep your arms and hands loose, letting them swing forward and back with the momentum, propelling you forward naturally.

- **Make it enjoyable.** Running workouts can be enjoyable. (OK, stop laughing. I'm being semiserious here.) Group runs can make training a social experience. The drawback is that their workout might be different from what you had planned, but you can always duck out if it's too long or run longer if it's too short.

For a Friend

Courtesy of Jamie Beecham.

Although Dion Harrison has always been an excellent athlete, running was certainly not his strong suit. Through college, he was a competitive backstroke swimmer and ranked at a national level in the United Kingdom in rugby and cricket. Still, when he was 17, he would have never considered doing something like running a marathon or competing in a triathlon . . . until tragedy struck.

"At that time, one of my close friends died of meningitis," says Dion. "So I decided to run the London Marathon in her honor and for a charity that would benefit the cause." Although running didn't come naturally to him, nor did he enjoy it, his aim was to be as competitive as he could, with a goal of running it under 4 hours. He completed it in 3:55, then ran three more London Marathons to bring his time down to 3:25.

But, as the charity opportunities of his marathon running dwindled, he decided to try to complete a triathlon. With his excellent swimming ability, he knew he could be competitive. In 2003, he decided on an unlikely goal for a beginner but one he thought would garner him significant charity sponsorship in memory of his friend: to finish the Ironman Lanzarote. He completed the race—his first triathlon—in an impressive time of 12:47.

Since the Lanzarote, Dion has focused primarily on the Ironman distance and done very well, finishing the Ironman UK in 10:58 in 2005. In 2006, he went back to the London Marathon and shattered his previous best with a 2:49 finish. Dion had several top five finishes in 2007, including a third-place finish at the Ironman 70.3 Worlds in Clearwater. His progress continued in 2008 with a 9:54 finish at the Ironman World Championship in Kona, Hawaii and a first-place finish in his age group at the ITU Long Distance Triathlon World Championships.

Despite his constant drive to push himself farther and faster, Dion always keeps his close friend in mind when he competes in a triathlon. "My friend is the reason I got into running and further along into triathlon."

Finding the Shoe That Fits

In the classic running book, *The Complete Book of Running*, New York City Marathon organizer Fred Lebow quotes a sports medicine podiatrist as saying, "Running shoes are like lovers. There is no one type for everyone, but when you find yours, you're set for life. Stick with it."

Finding the right shoe for the unique size, shape, and structure of your feet is one of the primary steps you need to take to cut down on foot problems. However, finding the perfect fit can be daunting. Invariably, questions regarding running gait arise. Should you get a shoe that will control your overpronation (when your foot rolls inward too much)? What if you need something that controls oversupination (when your foot rolls outward too much)?

"Most runners are obsessed with whether they supinate or pronate," says Dr. George Tsatsos, a sports medicine physician with a specialty in podiatry and a consultant to the American Running and Fitness Association. "A little bit of supination or pronation is normal, but many runners walk into a shoe store and buy shoes based on an incorrect self-diagnosis. This can result in buying the wrong shoe for your feet and the subsequent foot problems that come with that." Supination and pronation are caused by the shape of your foot, the amount of your arch, and your running technique. The important thing to remember is that you need to find the right shoe for your particular gait.

Here are some shopping recommendations that Dr. Tsatsos says will help you find the best-fitting pair of running shoes for your feet:

- Look for uneven pressure points when you're trying on your new shoes, especially in the toe area.
- Make sure the heel support is relatively stiff and firm.
- After lacing the shoe correctly, check for any excess movement or looseness.

"When you go to shop for a new shoe, make sure that you go during the middle or end of the day," adds Dr. Lawrence Burns, a sports medicine podiatrist. "You should do this because your feet swell somewhat after prolonged pressure from standing and walking. This will ensure that you get the right size shoe. If the salesperson measures your foot, make sure you are standing."

Other factors to consider are whether you will be running on the road, on trails, or both. There are specialty running shoes today that cater to trail running. In addition, different manufacturers vary in how they size their shoes, so best to visit your local pro running shop rather than buy from a running catalog. Best of all, bring in your old running shoes and an experienced sales associate should be able to tell what kind of shoe you need based on where the greatest amount of wear is on your soles.

Running in the Heat

Although heat can be a problem in any of the three sports, it is the biggest obstacle in running. Water is a natural coolant during a swim, and the wind in cycling does provide some cooling effect (although most of the tips here also apply to cycling in the heat).

Running in searing heat can be unpleasant. The sun beats down on your sweaty brow, the humidity factor makes it feel as though you're breathing pea soup, and your running shoes stick to sizzling asphalt. Worst of all, running in high temperatures can be dangerous.

Obviously, running in the heat can also affect performance. In a research article titled "Impact of Weather on Marathon-Running Performance," published in *Medicine & Science in Sports & Exercise* (Ely et al. 2007), the authors sought to measure the effect of the weather on running. They found that even slight increases in temperature and humidity had significant effects on the finishing times of even highly trained professional female and male runners. For slower amateur runners (i.e., the rest of us) the study showed that the effects are even greater.

The key to performing better in the heat and avoiding these hot-weather dangers is careful planning and preparation. Abiding by these few common-sense running tips will keep you from being a summertime triathlon training casualty:

- **Become acclimatized.** When the mercury begins to soar, adjust your training pace. Too many triathletes expect to maintain the same intensity in their workouts without allowing their bodies to adapt to the heat. Your body will eventually adjust to the heat with regular exercise in hot conditions. Some of these heat adaptations include improved blood flow to the skin, higher heart rate, decreased perspiration, and less salt loss in sweat. This period of adjustment, or acclimatization, usually takes about 10 days of workouts strung together in similar conditions.
- **Avoid the ozone zone.** Perhaps the best way of beating the heat is avoiding it altogether. That means running early in the morning or later in the evening. Another variable is the air quality, which tends to worsen as the temperature rises. If you live in a congested area and are frequently forced to run in close proximity to traffic during midday hours, you could be hurting your health, not helping it.

RACING TIP

Any well-organized race will have aid stations on the run course where you can fill up with water or sports drinks. You should drink at every aid station (especially if it's hot), but competitors differ on whether to continue to run, or walk while drinking. Your choice should depend on your race goal. If time is not a big concern, a brief period of walking while you sip on Gatorade will help your legs recover. If you do decide to hydrate on the fly, grab the paper cup and squeeze the top of the cup to keep fluids from spilling. Squeeze the brim enough to form a V shape; this will form a funnel for easy drinking while running.

"Since your breathing increases dramatically when you exercise, you will breathe more harmful chemicals when exercising in a polluted environment," states a pamphlet on safe running published by the American Running and Fitness Association (ARFA). In one cited study, athletes who ran in a polluted area had three times the concentration of harmful chemicals in their bloodstreams than the average population in this area, equivalent to smoking 10 to 20 cigarettes a day. ARFA recommends running in the morning, when the air quality is best, or after rush hour. Ozone levels begin to increase soon after dawn and peak at around noon and early afternoon, so avoid running at midday.

- **Wear light clothing.** Choose your clothing carefully. Wear light colors and use a sleeveless running singlet or lightweight T-shirt. Men should never run without a top (unless in a shaded area) to avoid sunburn. Use running shorts with slits on the side for ventilation and made from materials such as Coolmax that wick away moisture.

- **Protect yourself from the sun.** One of the biggest dangers in being outside is the effects of sun on the skin. UV light causes irreversible skin damage and skin aging, not to mention the increased likelihood of skin cancer. In addition to the previous clothing tips, here is some more advice from the Skin Cancer Foundation:

  1. Apply a sunscreen with sun protection factor (SPF) of 15 or greater before every run, even on overcast days.
  2. Wear sunglasses that shield your eyes from harmful UV rays.
  3. Use a visor or hat with a mesh top to allow for heat dissipation from the top of your head.
  4. Beware of reflective surfaces such as sand, concrete, and water, which can reflect more than half the sun's rays onto your skin.

- **Drink plenty of fluids.** Avoid dehydration and heat illness by staying properly hydrated. Drink eight ounces of water or a sports drink every 15 minutes while you run. Either plan your route so that you have a water fountain or convenience store stop along the way (make sure you bring money), or bring some fluid with you. I wouldn't recommend carrying a water bottle in your hand as you run (it throws off your stride, and it's damned annoying).

But plenty of products, such as water belts, water bottle holders, and the Camelbak, make it easier to bring along some fluids.

Hydrate before and after each run. If you drive to a running trail, drink fluids on the way there and bring along a small cooler so that your favorite carbohydrate beverage is nice and cold after your run. Because dehydration is potentially fatal and typically misunderstood among novice runners, you'll find further information on fluids and avoiding heat illnesses in chapter 8.

Your Running Repertoire

If you think running is just a matter of keeping your legs moving, you need to expand your training repertoire to include a variety of runs: for example, fartlek, track intervals, hill workouts, and good old LSD (no, not the drug; it stands for long slow distance). You also have trail runs, flat runs, hilly runs, short runs, long runs, tempo runs—all kinds of ways to put one foot in front of the other.

It's good to know your choices, but not every training technique mentioned here is a good option for the beginner or newcomer. The following sections describe a few types of workouts that might help you train wisely and make sure you've got something left in your legs at the end of a race.

Long Slow Distance

Once a week, do long, steady runs at a pace that could be considered "comfortably hard." (Isn't that an oxymoron?) Run at a pace that you can maintain for an hour without undue respiratory stress—in other words, without sounding as though you're having a heart attack. Practically speaking, this run is the typical long, conversational run that groups often get together for on a weekend morning. (After which, they partake in a ritualistic pancakes, sausage, and scrambled eggs platter at Denny's.)

Some experts recommend working at what you perceive to be 60 to 70 percent of your perceived maximum effort, but some research has indicated that a range of 50 to 60 percent is just as beneficial. If you're like me and have no idea what that means, your best bet is to listen for your breath—if you can hear yourself laboring, you're going too fast. This low-intensity approach, coupled with a long continuous effort, is ideal for developing the cardiorespiratory system, improving blood flow to active muscles, and building overall fitness and strength.

Tempo Running

This training is running at a pace that you can maintain for 20 to 30 minutes and that is 15 to 20 seconds slower than your fastest 10K pace. Sometimes runners refer to these runs as "lactic acid threshold" workouts.

Tempo runs take your body to the edge of what's called your lactate threshold, which is the point where lactic acid begins accumulating in the blood at a more rapid rate than normal. You might have experienced going beyond your lactate threshold

Keep your training repertoire fresh with different kinds of running, from relaxed long runs to intervals on a track.

when climbing a hill or getting on a stair-climbing machine and feeling a burn in your thighs. Tempo runs push your threshold further and further away so that eventually your body is able to tolerate a faster pace without lactic acid buildup. If physiological jargon scares you, think of these runs as performance boosters that help to increase the pace your body can maintain for a distance.

Run your tempo runs at slightly slower than the speed at which you'd race the same distance. Tempo runs stress your body to your lactate threshold. Keep in mind that hills, uneven footing, and strong winds can affect intensity, so try to run tempo runs on a flat, even course.

Fartlek

Fartlek is a Swedish word meaning speed-play. These medium-distance runs include random and relatively short bursts of speed in the middle of a run, thrown in to help break up the monotony. In addition to the mental break fartlek runs provide, they are also a good way of playing with your body, getting a feel for a certain pace, and assessing how quickly you recover from the increased effort. A fartlek run can be almost anything, from running hard every other block to racing your training partner to the next water fountain or light pole. Keep these bursts of speed under control; they should not dominate your workout as do the bursts in the more-regulated interval training (see the later section on this topic). The speed-play should be sparse, relatively short, and never done as an all-out sprint.

Hilly Workouts

Running hills is a great way to intensify your workouts. Running uphill is an excellent workout for your hamstring muscles and running downhill increases coordination skills and strengthens vital quadriceps muscles. As with any higher-intensity training tool, however, you should approach running hills cautiously. Without a proper running base, a safe course, and the right technique, hill running can cause injuries such as shin splints, calf tears, and knee soreness. If you are ready for hill workouts, pay special attention to your uphill and downhill running technique. Proper form will help you finish these workouts safely.

Here are some quick technique tips for running uphill:

- Shorten your stride.
- Lean into the hill.
- Keep your arms low for better balance.
- Pump your arms (but don't exaggerate the motion).

When running downhill, follow these guidelines:

- Lengthen your stride.
- Don't put the brakes on by leaning backward or shortening your stride (unless you have to).
- Keep your arms higher for better balance.

Interval Training (Not Recommended for Beginners)

Interval workouts are a form of speedwork, comprised of high-intensity workouts to improve performance. I don't recommend speedwork for the beginning runner; the stress and strain these workouts put on your legs is tremendous. Intervals require a greater foundation of training than novices typically possess.

As was mentioned in the swimming chapter, intervals are repeated, short bursts of speed over a measured distance. Running intervals are usually done on a track, with recovery periods of either walking or relaxed jogging between each interval. The purpose of interval running is to increase your maximum oxygen uptake, and the faster running teaches your body to be more biomechanically efficient.

Running With Troy

Troy Jacobson has been coaching triathletes of every level since 1992 and is widely considered to be one of the most prolific and established coaches in the sport. He has participated in over 150 triathlons, garnering more than 40 victories. Troy coaches triathletes through his Web site, www.coachtroy.com. "I've got a good mix of beginners, middle-of-the-packers, and professionals that I coach," he says. "I really enjoy working with triathletes training for their first race. My goal is to get them on the right track from the start."

Troy loves to race long distances. He has competed in over 150 races in his career including 15 Ironman events and over 25 half-Ironman events. Although triathlon is his sport, Troy is also a talented distance runner in his own right. He holds a PR (personal record) time of 2:31 in the marathon. I've asked Troy to answer some common questions novice triathletes ask about run training.

Expert Q & A

There are always a ton of questions on beginning triathletes' minds when they come to me for running advice. I'm glad to be able to answer here some of the most common questions, which I've put together from my experience. The questions come from beginners ranging from little athletic background to those who have more running experience.

Q: What can I do to improve how I feel coming off the bike?

A: First, make sure you put in a solid base of running. If you're not a huge fan of running, you might try to avoid it as much as possible, but that kind of approach will do you in at the end of a triathlon. Second, brick workouts that combine biking and running are very helpful. (You'll find more on bricks in the next chapter.) Third, during the race, take shorter steps in the first half mile (.8 km) to minimize the discomfort and stretch out the leg muscles. Gradually increase your stride until you're running normally.

Q: How much distance should I put in each week?

A: Most of my beginners are training for a sprint- or Olympic-distance race and average about 15 to 20 miles (24 to 32 km) a week. However, I don't recommend you go by miles or kilometers as much as time. Time is a more controllable variable and much easier to measure.

Q: I've heard so much about intervals. Should I be doing these kinds of workouts?

A: Interval workouts are for more advanced and performance-oriented runners. If you're just beginning and simply want to finish a race, run at an aerobic pace, which means a comfortable intensity. The most common running mistake I see triathletes make is running too hard. This "no pain, no gain" mentality is just ridiculous. Many beginners I coach think that they need to do intense runs, like intervals, to benefit. That's simply not true. Sometimes impatience and competitiveness can get in the way, too. I have a few triathletes who not only want to get fit, they want to get faster in a hurry, which normally takes years of advanced training. If your competitive juices are flowing, it's important to realize that you need to take it one step at a time to avoid injury and progress safely.

Q: What's a comfortable pace?

A. It's different for everyone. I work one-on-one with my athletes to find where their comfort zone is. But generally, if you take a perceived exertion level of 1 to 10 (10 is your maximum effort for a 3-mile, or 5K, run), I find aerobic running usually falls somewhere around 6.

Q: I'm always getting injured. What can I do to avoid injury?

A: I get many beginners who are either coming back from an injury or have chronic leg problems from running. Sports medicine is not my area of expertise, so I refer athletes having injury problems to a sports clinic in my area that offers a sophisticated computerized running gait analysis. Using digital cameras, they take a close look at how you run and how your stride might be contributing to injury, and then provide recommendations. If you have a similar facility in your area, I strongly advise that you use it. If not, at least go to a running specialty store to find the right shoe and try to do most of your workouts on trails and other soft surfaces.

chapter 7

Training for All Three

If you can create a training program that works for you, one based on sound, scientific, commonsense principles, then you'll be way ahead of the pack.

—Paula Newby-Fraser

How's your balancing act? At work, are you good at juggling two or more projects or tasks at one time, or do you find yourself leaning toward one and neglecting the others? Do you have a good balance between your family and career, or does your home life suffer because you don't spend enough time with your spouse and kids?

What do all these questions have to do with triathlon training? Well, in many ways, your success in putting together three distinct exercise activities into one solid training program will depend on how skilled you are at balancing. Sure, we'll go over some practical tips in this chapter, such as how to create a functional training schedule and how to bike off the swim and run off the bike. Ultimately, however, your success will hinge on your mental approach to the sport and how well you balance your training and your life.

Take a quick mental inventory of your success in balancing other aspects of your life. Do you have a tendency to take things a bit too far? If that's the case, maybe your learning experience with triathlon will improve much more than just your fitness.

Triathlon Training Dos and Don'ts

Good training is not just about listening to your body, although that's certainly important. It's also about listening to your family, and your boss, and the voice in your head that keeps telling you not to go overboard on your training. The following list of dos and don'ts will help you get the most out of your triathlon training:

- **Do add variety.** Don't do the same thing all the time—reach for new goals and challenges. Change your running course, or better yet, take the family to a weekend getaway, preferably somewhere where you can still get in some training. That way you can combine family values with your triathlon goal.

- **Don't sacrifice your family or career.** Stick to your priorities. Triathlon training should be a solid addition to a well-balanced lifestyle, not an obsession that hinders your family life or puts your career in danger. Besides, your chances of succeeding in triathlon—whatever that means to you—will greatly increase if you have the support of your family and coworkers.

- **Do be realistic about your available time.** There's nothing worse than constantly checking your watch during a workout. Part of the reason for working out is for stress relief, so why not schedule your workouts during a time of day when you won't feel hurried? Overestimating how much time you have to train can lead to feeling rushed and frustrated and can also make you go faster than you should be going.

- **Don't be inflexible.** Don't be so rigid in your training that you endanger your health or neglect other priorities. If your training schedule seems to be too hard on your body, rethink your approach and build in more recovery days, or cut the distance or intensity.

- **Do follow the hard/easy rule.** Working at a high intensity all the time increases your chance of injury. Give your body time to recover, especially from hard or long runs, with easy workouts on the day following a hard one.

Training in Phases

In chapter 2, we looked at various training phases recommended for the beginner. As you recall, training in phases (or cycles) allows you to focus on one component of your training for an extended time. This type of training ensures that you progress safely and gradually. After all, there's no such thing as overnight fitness.

The following is a more complete description of each of these phases, followed by some sample workout schedules that incorporate all three disciplines. These

If your family is willing, bring them along on shorter workouts. The change can help break up the monotony of daily runs.

sample training schedules differ according to each phase. If you haven't already divided your training schedule into these phases, do so now. Or if you'd like, photocopy the blank training grids at the end of this book and use them to plan your training phases.

View these schedules as templates or general guidelines to setting up your unique training plan. Devising a training schedule can be frustrating without guidelines. Add to this the anxiety of recurring questions about diet, equipment choices, and the optimal race schedule, and things can get pretty complicated.

You'll notice only the sprint and Olympic distances are covered here. That's because the vast majority of beginners and novice triathletes do (and should) start at the sprint distance and progress to the Olympic distance. Some athletes, especially endurance veterans who already are proficient in one or more of the three disciplines, choose to start with an Olympic-distance race. (Although there are several awe-inspiring cases of newcomers taking on the half-Ironman or Ironman distances, I don't recommend it.)

These training templates are loosely based on the key workout method pioneered by eight-time Ironman triathlon champion Paula Newby-Fraser. If you're interested in not just finishing a triathlon, but doing well, this approach includes one workout in each sport that is designed to achieve the objective of each phase.

Of course, feel free to substitute similar workouts that result in the same training effect. You'll also find some recommendations on alternative workouts and ideas to mix things up a bit.

Some workouts are optional. Gauge how you feel on those days. If you notice signs of overtraining, such as elevated heart rate, moodiness, and joint fatigue, back off and take a recovery day. It's a good idea anyway to take off at least one day a week to help you recover mentally and physically. In the following sample workout schedules, you'll notice that Monday is earmarked for recovery. That's because, in most cases, the longest or hardest workouts will fall on weekends. Mondays allow you to recover from these workouts and start fresh for another week of triathlon training.

Many of the swimming workouts focus on drills. That's because, as we discussed in chapter 4, a common mistake too many triathletes make is putting in too many laps without executing proper technique. Unlike running and biking, swimming depends heavily on technique. Remember, drills can help you unlearn bad habits and swim more efficiently.

The Initiation Phase (Beginners Only)

If you're starting from square one with little or no endurance training experience in either swimming, cycling, or running, make time in your training for getting your feet wet, literally and figuratively, in multisports. (If you have a good or above-average endurance training background in all three sports, congratulations! You get to skip to the next phase.)

This phase might try your patience, because you'll be learning at least one activity that you've never attempted before. For you to learn safely, workouts will usually be brief (though your muscles might feel as if they've gone a lot longer). This is a time for your body to adapt gradually to new activity and to overcome the inevitable discomforts that go with triathlon training. It might take you weeks to swim one lap without hugging the wall, ride three miles without feeling as though your rear end has been caned, and run around the block without feeling as though your lungs are going to explode. Be patient. Your body has a remarkable ability to adapt. Remember: Good things come to triathletes who are kind to their bodies.

Here are some things you should know about the initiation phase:

- This phase can last one to three months, depending on how quickly you learn and how well your body adapts.
- If you're new to swimming, this phase will consist of a beginner's swimming class and at least two to three workouts per week on your own to perform drills learned in that class.
- If you're new to cycling or running, this phase will consist of short, easy workouts with plenty of recovery time in between.
- The patience of a saint is required, especially if you're just learning to swim.

The following sample workout schedules are examples of initiation training for beginners to swimming, cycling, and running.

Initiation to Swimming Sample Workout Schedule

Mon	Off
Tue	**Key workout:** beginners' swim class
Wed	Practice drills learned in this week's class for 20 min
Thu	Off
Fri	Practice drills learned in this week's class for 30 min
Sat	Off
Sun	Practice drills learned in this week's class for 30 min

Initiation to Cycling Sample Workout Schedule

Mon	Off
Tue	15 to 20 min of easy spinning
Wed	Off
Thu	15 to 20 min of easy spinning
Fri	Off
Sat	**Key workout:** 30 min of easy spinning with a rest stop halfway (if necessary)
Sun	Off

Initiation to Running Sample Workout Schedule

Mon	Off
Tue	2 min of easy running and 1 min of walking; do this five times
Wed	Off
Thu	2 min of easy running and 1 min of walking; do this five times
Fri	Off
Sat	Off
Sun	**Key workout:** 5 min of easy running and 2 min of walking; do this two times

The following are some things to keep in mind during this phase:

- If you are new to more than one sport, you will need to combine two or three schedules into one that works for you.
- For a sport in which the initiation phase is not required, refer to the Base Training Workout Schedule on page 99 for guidance.
- If you're a beginning swimmer, be sure to work on the weekly lessons and drills independently of your swimming class.
- You'll know when you're ready to transition out of this phase into the next when you seem to recover faster from workouts, you developed some proficiency in technique or skill (swimming with your head in the water, cycling with clipless pedals, feeling relaxed while running), and you feel strong enough emotionally and physically.

The Base Phase

When construction contractors build a home or office building, they spend significant time ensuring that the foundation is solid and stable. Once that's done, the rest of the building goes up relatively quickly.

The same can be said of base training for endurance sports. This phase might take the longest. But the long-term rewards are injury prevention, greater performance, and healthy balance. It's worth noting that if your goal is just to finish a race, your workouts might consist almost entirely of base training. That's fine. As long as you have a solid foundation, just finishing is a realistic goal.

Here are some things to keep in mind about base training:

- It can last from three to six months, depending on your current conditioning, skills, and the distance for which you are training.
- This phase consists mainly of long workouts done at a slow pace.
- Focus on gradual increases of workout length of no more than 10 percent per week, a rule that is especially crucial for running (discussed in chapter 6) and helps avoid common overtraining injuries.

Refer to the sample workout schedule for the sprint distance on the next page.

The following are some training tips for this phase:

- Conduct your running and cycling workouts at a conversational, easy pace; if your breathing is labored, you're going too fast.
- If your current workout in a given sport isn't within the time ranges given in the sample workout schedule, gradually increase your training using the 10 percent rule explained in chapter 6.
- Remember, spinning means keeping your RPM at 85 to 95. If you don't have a bike computer or one with a cadence feature, ride in a gear that isn't too hard.

- Run on soft surfaces, such as wilderness trails, to avoid knee problems. Watch for dips in trails and chipmunk holes so you don't twist an ankle.
- Advanced options are provided if you've already established some fitness and skills in any of the three disciplines.

Base Training Sample Workout Schedule (Sprint Distance)

	Swimming	Cycling	Running
Mon	Off	Off	Off
Tue	30 min of drill practice	30 min of easy spinning	Off
Wed	Off	30-45 min of easy spinning	15 min of easy running
Thu	**Key workout:** 10 × 50 yard intervals w/ 30 sec rest **Advanced option:** 10 × 75 yard interval w/ 20 sec rest	Off	(optional) 20 min tempo run
Fri	30 min of drill practice	(optional) 30 min of easy spinning	(optional) 20 min tempo run
Sat	Off	**Key workout:** work up to a 60 min ride **Advanced option:** Do the ride on a slightly hilly course, but maintain a steadily moderate to slow pace on climbs	Off
Sun	(optional) 400-meters easy swimming with some drill sets	Off	**Key workout:** work up to a 30-45 min easy run with 2 min walking breaks (if necessary) **Advanced option:** 45 min easy run with no walking breaks

The Speed and Technique Phase

You may not be at all concerned with how fast you stroke, pedal, or put one foot in front of the other. Good for you. If your next triathlon will be your first, the best thing you can do for yourself is dismiss any expectations you have of finishing by a certain time. Do it simply to finish. Period.

"Good. Now release and repeat."

But if you have a few multisport events under your belt, speed and technique workouts can help you hone your skills for safer, more efficient training. If that doesn't motivate you, how about the prospect of finishing a triathlon without feeling like you've just been run over by a steamroller?

That said, don't overemphasize these workouts. Speedwork, such as interval training on a running track, can wreak havoc on your body. It's a frequently confusing and misunderstood topic, particularly for the novice, and can lead to injury. In summary, if your goal is to improve your race time, then this phase is key. If your goal is simply to complete your first triathlon, skip it.

Here are some things to keep in mind about speed and technique training:

- It can last from three weeks to several months, depending on your current conditioning and performance goals.
- This phase consists of a select few (one per week in each sport, max) high-intensity workouts designed to increase cardiorespiratory and mechanical efficiency.

- Speedwork can easily lead to injury if you haven't completed your base training. Don't progress to speedwork until you have been doing long, slow workouts for at least three months.

See the following sample workout schedule for speed and technique training. The following are some workout tips for speed and technique training:

- Always ease into a workout. Make sure you warm up properly before long or hard sessions.
- I've provided advanced options if you've already established some fitness and skills in any of the three disciplines.

Speed and Technique Phase
Sample Workout Schedule (Sprint Distance)

	Swimming	Cycling	Running
Mon	Off	Off	Off
Tue	**Key workout:** 10 × 50 yard intervals w/ 15 sec rest **Advanced option:** 10 × 75 yard intervals w/ 10 sec rest	30 min of easy spinning	Off
Wed	30 min of drill practice	Off	15 min of easy running
Thu	Off	**Key workout:** 45 min ride on a challenging, hilly course **Advanced option:** 45 min ride on a challenging, hilly course with sprints to the top of each hill. Coast downhill to recover between hills.	Off
Fri	400-meters easy swimming and 15 min of drill sets	(optional) 30 min of easy spinning	20 min tempo run
Sat	Off	60 min easy ride	Off
Sun	(optional) 400-meters easy swimming with some drill sets	Off	**Key workout:** 30 min fartlek run **Advanced option:** Track intervals: run a slow 1-mile warm-up; run six quarter-mile intervals at your 5K pace with 30 sec recovery after each; run a slow 1-mile cool-down

The Race Simulation Phase

Among the biggest concerns for the beginner looking to complete his or her first triathlon is the mystery that awaits all first-time triathletes on that fateful day. Questions inevitably arise, many of them associated with transitioning from one sport to the other and the transitions' effects on the body:

- How am I going to feel coming out of the water?
- How do I handle the transitions?
- What if my muscles cramp going from the bike to the run?

That last question is a legitimate concern. Most triathletes agree that the toughest transition is from bike to run, particularly if your cycling leg has been especially intense or hilly. Even if you've taken it easy on the bike, you might find yourself starting the run feeling like the gears are turning, but you're going nowhere. Prepare yourself for this unsettling sensation during the bike-to-run transition, but also realize that all you need is a little practice, some encouragement, and confidence.

Race training is designed not necessarily to improve your performance in a race (although that might be an incidental effect) but to give you the confidence and encouragement you need. Workouts known as "bricks" combine two sports in a single session and are instrumental to racing success. By completing workouts that simulate what you will experience during a race, the shroud of mystery surrounding your upcoming first triathlon will evaporate. If you're looking to improve upon previous performances or lengthen your distances, race simulation training will help you do that as well.

Here are some things to keep in mind about this training phase:

- It can last one to two months, depending on your current conditioning and race goals.
- This phase consists of workouts designed to simulate transitions and race conditions, such as bricks that combine two activities in succession and certain key workouts.
- Race simulation can help you hone your transitioning skills.

See page 103 for examples of race simulation workouts for the sprint distance. Here are some additional things to keep in mind for race simulation workouts:

- Notify the lifeguard on duty before your open-water swim.
- Do your bike time trial on a course with little or no traffic or stoplights.
- If you'd like, substitute the bike time trial with a fast and competitive group ride.
- For your brick workouts, prepare a mock transition area, making the transition as you would in a race.

Race Simulation Phase Sample Workout Schedule (Sprint Distance)

	Swimming	Cycling	Running
Mon	Off	Off	Off
Tue	**Brick:** 500-yard swim (open water strongly recommended) with transition to bike and 30 min of easy spinning		Off
Wed	40 min of drill practice	Off	15 min of easy running
Thu	Off	**Key workout:** 30 min time trial ride at or near race pace	Off
Fri	400-meters easy swimming and drill sets	(optional) 45 min of easy spinning	20 min tempo run
Sat	30 min of drill practice	Off	Off
Sun	Off	**Brick:** 45 min easy ride followed by an immediate transition to a 20 min tempo run **Advanced brick:** 30 min hilly or fast-paced ride followed by an immediate transition to a 20 min tempo run	

- The advanced brick workout is a secondary option. If you complete the brick workouts with little or no difficulty on several occasions, try this somewhat harder (though shorter) workout. This session should accurately reproduce how you might feel coming off the bike in the race—just make sure you take the run nice and easy.

- Drink plenty of fluids—doing so will minimize the chances of cramping during the bike-to-run transition.

The Tapering Phase

Tapering means decreasing your activity in the days or weeks prior to an athletic event. This gives your body time to recover from the previous months of training so that you feel mentally fresh and your muscles are primed for racing.

Although there is much debate about the "perfect" tapering schedule, it really depends on how fast your body recovers from training, how long you've been training, and what you are training for. And although there might be some disagreement about how to taper, experts do concur that you need to taper to perform your best. After all, the last thing you want to do is start a race with your legs feeling sore.

The value of tapering is something that endurance athletes have known for a long time. Nevertheless, you still hear stories of the competitor who insisted on putting in one last hard workout the day before a race, only to find himself exhausted at the starting line.

Here are some things you should know about tapering:

- For a sprint- or Olympic-distance race, tapering usually encompasses the week prior to your event goal.
- Tapering consists of shorter, easy workouts; it might also incorporate more rest days.
- Tapering has benefits for both the first-timer and the veteran triathlete.

The following are a few tips to help you feel fresh on race day:

- Increase your consumption of carbohydrates during tapering.
- Get plenty of sleep and relaxation.
- If you get a massage, make sure to schedule it at least a week to five days before the race to avoid possible soreness from deep tissue work.

It doesn't make much difference what your workouts consist of in the week prior to an event. What does make a difference is how much you do and how hard you do it. That's why the following tapering charts provide a recommended total workout time (the total time spent on any one or combination of three sports in one day).

The first chart is for tapering over a full week, and the other is for tapering three days prior to an event. If you tend to take a long time to recover from a workout, it's best if you go with a one-week taper. If you tend to recover pretty quickly, then you'll probably do fine tapering three days before the event.

One-Week Taper

Day 1	40 min
Day 2	Complete rest
Day 3	40 min
Day 4	20 min
Day 5	20 min
Day 6	Complete rest
Day 7	Race day

Half-Week Taper

Day 1	40 min
Day 2	20 min
Day 3	Complete rest
Day 4	Race day

"The biggest and most common mistake is to go into an event overtrained," says Dr. Jeff Zachwieja, principal scientist at the Gatorade Sports Science Institute (GSSI). "If you haven't gotten the rest your muscles need to repair the micro damage that occurs during training, you will significantly hinder their ability to store enough glycogen for what you need."

In most cases, sticking to an appropriate tapering schedule that lowers both distance and intensity in the days and weeks prior to an event will ensure that your muscles are in good shape.

Bricks: A Life Lesson

Courtesy of Joe Albert.

When Joe Albert started competing in triathlons in 1996, the toughest part of each race for him was the first mile of the run. Having just made inroads into endurance exercise in the previous year, he found he had a natural talent for running. Unfortunately, that talent went down the tubes every time he came off the bike. "It was just excruciating," says the 42-year-old resident of Plainfield, Illinois. "It was just mentally and physically tough for me, and when I got off the bike I just couldn't run like I knew I could."

With average mile times (splits) hovering around 7:30 for his triathlon run leg (a pace he considered slow), Joe set out to bring those times down. He learned from triathlon training books about bricks and began practicing one bike-to-run workout once a week. The results? During his second year of triathlon competition, his average triathlon run splits have come down to under 6-minute miles, a dramatic 90-second-per-mile improvement.

"I think most people have a problem getting into a good running stride after cycling," says Joe. "I figure if I can get into that stride right away, as opposed to a mile or two later, I can have a competitive advantage. Bricks definitely help me do that."

More recently, a health scare with a heart valve has kept him sidelined from triathlon, but he hopes to pick up on his brick training now that he's gotten the medical green light. In addition, his autistic daughter has gladly resulted in a reprioritization of his life.

"My life has changed dramatically since I've had to address the heart valve issue and run interference with my beautiful daughter," says Joe. "I guess triathlon training, such as bricks, teaches you to juggle things, which is also a life lesson."

Going for Olympic Glory

Although the sprint distance is perfect for the beginner or time-limited triathlete, the Olympic distance is ideal for those who want to push the endurance envelope beyond the two-hour boundary. It is also a good stepping-stone after completing a few sprint-distance races.

Following are a set of sample workout schedules for the Olympic distance. Once again, they are divided into phases, so most of the same principles and tips from the sprint-distance workouts apply. They are similar to the sprint-distance sample workouts (although obviously the distances are longer) with one notable exception: The tapering phase includes only one option, a full week's taper (see page 108). Because the training distances are greater for an Olympic-distance race, a full week's taper (as opposed to a half-week taper) will give your body the time it needs to recover and feel fresh on the starting line.

Base Training Sample Workout Schedule (Olympic Distance)

	Swimming	Cycling	Running
Mon	Off	Off	Off
Tue	30 min of drill practice	45 min of easy spinning	Off
Wed	Off	60 min of easy spinning	25 min of easy running
Thu	**Key workout:** 10 × 100 yard intervals w/ 15 sec rest **Advanced option:** 10 × 100 yard intervals w/ 10 sec rest	Off	(optional) 30 min tempo run
Fri	30 min of drill practice	(optional) 45 min of easy spinning	25 min easy run
Sat	Off	**Key workout:** 90 min easy ride **Advanced option:** 120 min easy ride	Off
Sun	(optional) 800-meters easy swimming with some drill sets	Off	**Key workout:** Work up to 60 min to 90 min slow distance run with 5 min walking break (if necessary) **Advanced option:** 75 min slow distance run, no walking breaks

Speed and Technique Phase Sample Workout Schedule (Olympic Distance)

	Swimming	Cycling	Running
Mon	Off	Off	Off
Tue	**Key workout:** 10 × 100 yard intervals w/ 10 sec rest	45 min of easy spinning	Off
Wed	30 min of drill practice	Off	25 min of easy running
Thu	Off	**Key workout:** 60 min ride on a challenging, hilly course	Off
Fri	800-meters easy swimming and 15 minute drill sets	45 min of easy spinning (optional)	30 min tempo run
Sat	Off	90 min easy ride	Off
Sun	800-meters easy swimming with some drill sets (optional)	Off	**Key workout:** 40 min fartlek run

Race Simulation Phase Sample Workout Schedule (Olympic Distance)

	Swimming	Cycling	Running
Mon	Off	Off	Off
Tue	**Brick:** 1000-meter swim (open water strongly recommended) with transition to bike and 45 min of easy spinning		Off
Wed	40 min of drill practice	Off	25 min of easy running
Thu	Off	**Key workout:** 45-60 min time trial ride at or near race pace	Off
Fri	800-meters easy swimming and drill sets	60 min of easy spinning (optional)	30 min tempo run
Sat	30 min of drill practice	Off	Off
Sun	Off	**Brick:** 45 min hilly or fast-paced ride followed by an immediate transition to a 30 min easy run	

One-Week Taper (Olympic Distance)

Day 1	60 min
Day 2	Complete rest
Day 3	40 min
Day 4	30 min
Day 5	20 min
Day 6	Complete rest
Day 7	Race day

Your Triathlon Training Schedule

You'll find some blank triathlon training grids in the back of the book, one for each phase. You can duplicate these grids and fill them in with your personal training schedules. Note: If you need to go through an initiation period in one or two activities, integrate those workouts with your base training in the others. If you are new to swimming, biking, and running, plan a separate workout schedule based entirely on the initiation phase before you begin base training.

PART III

Tri-ing Your Best

There's a whole lot more to triathlons than just training. Being the best tri-athlete you can be depends on other important factors. Nutrition, injury prevention, and knowing what to expect for your upcoming race are key variables in your multisport experience. And, finally, figuring out just how triathlon fits into everything else in your life is just as relevant to your success as all that technical know-how.

chapter 8

Fueling Up for Triathlon

If an athlete's training has a fixed schedule, but the eating doesn't, the athlete will suffer.

—Dr. Dan Benardot

When you think of food, fuel might be the last thing you think about. Yet what you put into your body greatly affects your energy level and, if you're training for triathlons, your performance. So, food is fuel, but what's the right kind of fuel?

Sports nutrition is a field that addresses the unique nutritional needs of active people. Nutritional frontiers are being charted every day as competitive triathletes demand more from their bodies and learn how good nutrition enables them to reach higher levels of performance. But sports nutrition isn't just for competitive triathletes; it's about the dietary needs of active people, such as you, who are delving into the challenging activity of triathlon.

Proper nutrition means meeting your daily caloric requirement and providing your body with the nutrients it needs for the growth, support, and repair of tissue. That might sound simple, but without some basic knowledge, sports nutrition can be a confusing maze of scientific terminology and theory. To help you better understand the link between eating and triathlon training, this chapter presents scientific facts and answers—in everyday language—the most commonly asked questions on sports nutrition.

Carbohydrate Loading

You've probably heard of carbohydrate loading, but for many people, the process of converting carbohydrate into energy is shrouded in mystery. The following sections provide a few facts about carbohydrate.

Carbohydrate: Our Prime Energy Source

Energy from food comes in three forms: carbohydrate, protein, and fat. Some of these fuels are stored in your body so that muscles and organs can use them as an immediate source of energy. Foods that you eat just before or during exercise also can fuel muscles.

Of these three fuels, carbohydrate is the most important nutrient for working muscles. It is the primary energy source for most physical activity and is burned more efficiently than protein or fat. Research has shown that energy from carbohydrate can be released within exercising muscles up to three times as fast as the energy from fat.

The primary function of carbohydrate is to provide energy. The drawback is that the body can store only a limited supply of carbohydrate at any given time. Two hours or less of endurance exercise can deplete liver and muscle glycogen (stored carbohydrate) levels. Therefore, a high-carbohydrate diet is essential for performing at your best.

Carbohydrate has other important functions:

- It is the only fuel that the brain and nervous system can use effectively. Low carbohydrate stores can cause diminished concentration.
- Adequate amounts of carbohydrate help spare protein reserves needed for muscle growth, maintenance, and repair.
- Carbohydrate helps the body burn fat more efficiently.
- Many foods high in carbohydrate (such as whole grains, fruits, and vegetables) are also high in dietary fiber for better digestion and prevention of certain types of cancer.

Carbohydrate Intake

At least 60 percent of the average person's daily caloric intake should be composed of carbohydrate. For example, a person who needs 3,000 calories per day to sustain a healthy body weight should eat at least 1,800 calories from carbohydrate (or 450 grams of carbohydrate) per day.

Triathletes, especially those training for longer events, need more and should shoot for a carbohydrate intake of 65 to 70 percent (more on this later in this chapter). Even if you don't consider yourself a competitive triathlete, the foundation of your diet should be foods high in carbohydrate. A high-carbohydrate diet is vital for anyone who leads an active lifestyle and exercises on a near-daily basis, regardless of whether that person is focused on performance.

Also, glycogen depletion is cumulative; after a few days of eating a low-carbohydrate diet and working out regularly, you might start to feel stale and worn out. Finally, a low-carbohydrate diet sometimes translates to a high-fat diet. The potential health-related problems of a diet high in saturated fat have been well documented.

Rice, pasta, breads, cereals, fruits, vegetables, and whole grains are high in carbohydrate. Eating these foods is an excellent way to increase carbohydrate stores in the body. Carbohydrate can be consumed in solid, gel, or liquid form.

Timing Your Carbohydrate Servings

Besides eating a high-carbohydrate diet daily, the timing of meals is important. To maximize your performance, you need to follow some specific nutrition guidelines before, during, and after exercise.

1. Before exercise

   Benefits: Eating carbohydrate before exercise increases muscle glycogen (carbohydrate stores) and helps maintain normal blood sugar levels.

   Guidelines: Consume 75 or more grams of carbohydrate one to two hours before training. For example, one bagel and one cup of pasta total 75 grams of carbohydrate.

2. During exercise

   Benefits: During exercise, muscle and liver glycogen stores can become depleted, leading to a drop in blood sugar. This drop could result in headaches, dizziness, muscle weakness, fatigue, and reduced performance. Consuming carbohydrate during endurance exercise can postpone fatigue and prolong peak performance.

   Guidelines: Drink 4 to 10 ounces of a sports drink, such as Gatorade, every 15 to 20 minutes during exercise.

3. After exercise

   Benefits: After exercise, carbohydrate intake speeds muscle recovery by replenishing glycogen stores. There is a brief time frame immediately after exercise in which it is essential to replenish carbohydrate; this time frame is known as the carbohydrate window. Studies have shown that when athletes eat carbohydrate in the hours after endurance exercise, their muscles recover faster.

   Guidelines: Immediately after exercise, consume healthy, high-carbohydrate snacks, such as fruits, bagels and energy bars. After that, continue eating a high-carbohydrate diet for rapid recovery.

What about that carbo-loading stuff? Carbohydrate loading, or carbo-loading, is a nutrition strategy that increases muscle glycogen capacity in the days before an endurance event by boosting carbohydrate intake and decreasing training. We'll talk about carbo-loading and other race-week strategies in greater detail in chapter 10.

SAMPLE HIGH-CARBOHYDRATE MEALS

Here's a sampling of some high-carbohydrate meals. When you add it up, approximately 67 percent of your calories from these meals come from carbohydrate, 17 percent come from protein, and 16 percent come from fat.

Breakfast

4 slices whole-wheat toast: 69 calories per slice

1 tablespoon peanut butter: 94 calories

.75 cup Grape Nuts cereal: 87 calories

1 cup (240 mL) skim milk: 86 calories

1 cup strawberries: 46 calories

1 cup (240 mL) orange juice: 132 calories

Lunch

2 ounces (60 g) lean beef patty: 195 calories

1 whole-grain hamburger bun: 130 calories

1 cup low-fat pasta and chicken salad: 218 calories

1 apple: 55 calories

1 cup skim milk: 86 calories

Dinner

3 ounces (90 g) broiled chicken breast, skinless: 142 calories

1 cup brown rice pilaf: 216 calories

1 slice whole-wheat bread: 69 calories

1 teaspoon margarine: 34 calories

1.5 cups vegetable salad without dressing: 33 calories

1 tomato: 18 calories

1 tablespoon low-fat salad dressing: 37 calories

1 cup (240 mL) nonfat milk: 86 calories

1 cup (230 g) low-fat frozen yogurt: 199 calories

Healthy Snacks (Two to Four Times a Day)

1 ounce (30 g) whole-wheat pretzels: 103 calories

1 banana: 72 calories

1 cinnamon raisin bagel (option: low-fat cream cheese): 156 calories, add
32 calories with low-fat cream cheese

1 PowerBar: 230 calories

That Gooey Stuff

One of the biggest-selling sports nutrition products available on the triathlete market is carbohydrate gels. No, you don't splotch the stuff on your hair to be more aerodynamic. You eat this gooey mess, much as you would an energy bar or any sports supplement.

Gels are essentially sports drinks without the water. They are composed primarily of carbohydrate, though some include small amounts of protein. A few carbohydrate-gel producers throw in some other ingredients: minute amounts of caffeine, herbs, vitamins, and minerals. Gels typically come in small, convenient packets or tubes, which you can easily carry in a bicycle jersey or tucked in the side of your running shorts or under a cap.

The best use of gels is as a racing aid, especially in longer events. If you have stomach problems when you eat carbohydrate in the form of solids or sports drinks, you might find gels to be more digestible. Of course, as with anything you intend to try in a race, always test a gel product during a training session. Also, don't substitute gels for fluid intake; you still need to drink enough during workouts and races.

RACING TIP

Just where do you put those little gel packets or tubes during your bike or run? Well, fortunately, many neat gadgets have surfaced to hold gel products since they've become so popular. Any pro bicycle shop or triathlon race expo will offer everything from tiny holders that clip onto your running shorts waistband to gel flasks that resemble mini water bottles and attach to your bicycle frame. If you decide to carry a gel product with you under a cap or in your hand, make sure you don't litter the race course with empty gel packets.

Carbohydrate and Stomach Problems

Because high-carbohydrate foods are usually high in fiber, they fill the stomach and make you feel full, sometimes causing stomach distress or, possibly, excessive gas. If you experience these symptoms because of a high-carbohydrate diet, try eating more frequently than three meals a day. Consuming several high-carbohydrate snacks throughout the day, such as bagels, fruit, rice cakes, and butterless popcorn, can make it easier to meet your carbohydrate needs.

Another solution might be to consume a carbohydrate-loading and recovery drink. These drinks are designed for before or after exercise, or as a supplement to help boost daily carbohydrate intake. Active people and athletes sometimes find it difficult to consume a diet high in carbohydrate because of the high fiber content. Carbo-loading drinks are a convenient way to ingest large amounts of carbohydrate without having to consume enormous quantities of filling foods. However, your diet should not consist of a majority of these beverages; you need the complex carbs of nutritious foods such as fruits, vegetables, and grains.

Even if you don't feel hungry after a race, try to replenish your body's carbohydrate stores within 20 minutes of finishing.

The balance you get in your diet from eating a variety of foods high in carbohydrate and other nutrients is important, too. Unfortunately, balanced nutrition is often a low priority for many active people, and it's difficult to eat the perfect diet in today's hectic society. Some sports nutrition products contain a good balance of calories from carbohydrate, protein, and fat, and are fortified with vitamins and minerals to help supplement the weak spots in your diet. (You'll see more on sports nutrition products later in the chapter.)

CHOOSING ENERGY BARS

Energy bars have become very popular in recent years, and can be a reliable source of carbohydrate and balanced nutrition. But choose your bar carefully; many products make impressive claims that are without scientific basis. Some energy bars are high in fat and contain partially hydrogenated oils and other ingredients that are not nutritious. Check the food label on the wrapper before deciding whether the bar is a healthy choice.

After you've determined which bars are healthy snacks, test them out. This testing might take a while, because some brands have a variety of flavors. Find one that makes your taste buds tingle. If you think an energy bar tastes like rubber while you're standing still, it won't taste any better on the run.

Dispelling the Protein Myth

Protein is perhaps the most misunderstood nutrient. It's ironic that although many people worry about not getting enough of it, most Americans surpass the recommended daily intake of protein. For triathletes, studies have found that protein does play a role in faster recovery.

Role of Protein

The principal role of protein is to build and repair body tissues, including muscles, ligaments, and tendons. Protein also plays a part in producing enzymes and hormones, thus serving a regulatory function. Contrary to popular belief, protein is not a primary source of energy, even for athletes engaged in heavy training.

Protein can be used for energy, but it must first be converted to carbohydrate or fat. During the latter stages of an endurance event, such as a long-distance triathlon, when glycogen stores are depleted, protein can supply up to 15 percent of the calories burned (but if calorie and carbohydrate intake are adequate, protein usage could be much lower).

A recent study proves that a high-carbohydrate diet combined with a moderate amount of protein helps provide more sustained energy under aerobic conditions. However, when protein is lacking from an athlete's diet, the athlete isn't able to use carbohydrate for energy as effectively.

Studies also prove that endurance athletes do need more protein than the average person does. The type of exercise you perform can affect amino acid turnover and dictate protein requirements. Endurance exercise increases amino acid oxidation (breakdown). Resistance exercise enhances protein turnover and muscle synthesis; therefore both cardiovascular and strength training exercise increase protein requirements for athletes.

Protein and Amino Acids

Proteins are composed of individual units called amino acids. There are 20 different amino acids, 11 of which are produced by the body. The other 9 are called essential amino acids and are gained from the foods we eat. If we don't consume essential amino acids, our bodies will have difficulty producing certain proteins, and health and performance can suffer. The typical American diet usually supplies all the essential amino acids. Although there are many claims that amino acid supplements enhance muscle growth and physical performance, there is little sound scientific evidence to support these claims.

Your Protein Needs

The typical American diet contains 200 to 250 percent of the recommended daily intake of protein. So even if you think you need to double your consumption of protein, chances are pretty good that your diet already provides adequate protein. As a good rule of thumb, protein should make up about 15 percent of your daily caloric intake.

Some studies have confirmed that a small to moderate amount of protein intake after a long workout or race can help speed muscle recovery. A number of sports supplements have added protein to their products for this reason. An energy bar with a moderate amount of protein (10 to 20 grams) and a high-carbohydrate drink is a good postexercise meal.

The Fear of Fat

Ooh, the "F" word. Fat is perhaps the most feared of nutrients, yet it does play an important role in a triathlete's diet. Besides providing a stored form of energy, fat contributes to healthy skin and is part of the structure of many hormones and cell membranes. Fat also allows fat-soluble vitamins, such as A, D, E, and K, to be absorbed by your body. Although most people abhor the fat stored on their bodies, fat cushions and protects delicate internal organs, such as the kidneys and liver. Fat even performs a life-saving function by helping the body form blood clots to stop bleeding.

Too Much of a Good Thing

Overconsumption of fat poses two major problems. First, fat is a very concentrated source of energy, so small amounts of it provide many calories and can lead to weight gain and obesity. Second, a high-fat diet, particularly one high in saturated fat, can lead to heart disease and certain types of cancer. Chronic diseases related to high fat intake are associated with two of the ten leading causes of death in the United States. Most nutrition authorities promote a reduction of fat in the American diet from the current 40 to 45 percent to fewer than 30 percent of total calories from fat.

Long live the midnight fridge run.

Though current FDA guidelines recommend that 30 percent of daily calories come from fat, triathletes might want to lower their fat intake to 20 percent or less of their caloric intake so that a greater portion of their calories come from carbohydrate. But even triathletes need some fat in their diet to perform vital functions and promote the absorption of fat-soluble vitamins. Female triathletes with below normal body fat are likely to experience a disruption in their menstrual cycle and a related loss of calcium, making them more prone to stress fractures.

What You Can Do to Reduce Fat in Your Diet

Eating healthy shouldn't mean a drastic crash-course diet but rather a sustained effort over time to make intelligent choices:

- Watch out for hidden fat. Sweet foods such as bran muffins, doughnuts, cookies, cakes, and pies have more fat than sugar calories. Similarly, crackers, chips, and other snack foods are high in fat. If in doubt, read the food labels.
- Cut down on the sauces and toppings added to your food. Gravy, salad dressing, sour cream, butter, margarine, mayonnaise, and whipped cream are almost all fat. Even small amounts of these foods can boost the fat content of your diet.
- Buy low-fat dairy products. Nonfat milk has the same nutritional value as whole milk but no fat and half the calories. It also has more calcium than whole milk. Cottage cheese, yogurt, and frozen yogurt made from nonfat milk have this same advantage.
- Use low-fat cooking techniques such as broiling, grilling, and stir-frying, rather than deep-frying or pan-frying. If you eat out, ask how the food is prepared before ordering.
- Select lean cuts of meat, such as loin or round. The grade of meat is based on the fat content. Choice and prime grade are the highest in fat; the less-expensive select grade is the lowest in fat.
- Remove the visible fat from meat before cooking it and drain the grease from hamburger after frying it. Also, before eating poultry, remove the skin.
- Make most fats you eat come from unsaturated sources, such as avocados, nuts, and olives, and cooking in olive or canola oil, rather than unhealthy saturated fat.

Making Healthy Food Choices

Make the same commitment to healthy eating that you do to training. Reading and correctly interpreting the new food labels and the Food Guide Pyramid are two ways to become more aware of what you're putting in your mouth.

Weighty Inspiration: More Time

Courtesy of Marathon-Photos.com.

Inspiration to jump into triathlon can come from anywhere. And, in Toby Baxendale's case, it came from both a weight problem and a former Olympic cyclist.

At age 30, Toby was overweight, pushing 210 pounds (95 kg). "I employed some of the best chefs in town, which helped me create a very unhealthy person who was bordering on getting properly fat," he says.

As a successful businessman who employs 560 people in the United Kingdom to supply fish and meat to hotels, restaurants, contract caterers, stadiums, supermarkets, and even royal palaces, he found less success in being healthy. At first, inspiration to lose weight came when he saw the London Marathon in 1999 and embarked on a training program that got him to the finish line of the New York City Marathon that same year. After several more years of hard training, losing weight, and continuing to better his marathon time all the way down to an impressive 3:18, he found inspiration from a fellow local running club member, 65-year-old UK Olympic cyclist Brendan McKeon.

"Brendan was an extraordinary time-trial cyclist in the 1964 and 1968 Olympics, and I took inspiration from that fact that, at his age, he was still as fit as ever," says the resident of central Hertfordshire. He learned to swim, took up cycling, and continued running, finishing his first triathlon in 2005. As impressive was his 4:58 finishing time for his first race, the Vitruvian, which is just a few kilometers shy of a half-Ironman distance.

Now Toby has a full Ironman under his belt, many half Ironmans, and two Ironman 70.3 world championship finishes. Toby is also a part-time judge in the UK and an affiliate professor at the European School of Management, and he is happily married with three healthy children. What's his secret to time management?

"The trick is to be consistent in life and, above all, stop watching television. The tube is, at best, rubbish and, at worst, complete garbage. Not watching television frees up hours for other things, like triathlon training!"

Reading Food Labels

To help the American consumer better understand the contents of foods and make better dietary choices, the Food and Drug Administration requires that packaged foods include a Nutrition Facts label (see sample on next page). The label can also help people with health problems limit their intake of certain nutrients—fat, sugar, or salt, for instance—or increase consumption of others, such as fiber or calcium.

The food label is a good way to determine the nutritional value of packaged foods and is a general guideline for eating a healthy diet. But the triathlete must make several modifications when reading food labels:

- The Daily Values tell you how much of a day's recommended total allotment of nutrients is contained in the food. The percents of Daily Values are based on a 2,000-calorie diet, which is usually lower than the number of calories a physically active person needs to maintain weight and ingest the required amounts of nutrients. A better method is to calculate the grams of carbohydrate you need daily and aim for that amount.

- The Daily Values are based on a diet composed of 60 percent of calories from carbohydrate. Athletes who need to replace glycogen stores depleted during exercise should consider increasing their carbohydrate intake to 65 percent of their daily diet. For example, the athlete on a 3,500-calorie diet should consume 570 grams of carbohydrate daily.

- If you stick to the Daily Values, your daily caloric intake of fat will be 30 percent, a good target. But the health-conscious person might want to lower fat consumption to 20 percent of daily caloric intake.

- The bottom section of the food label lists the recommended daily intake of nutrients for a 2,000- and 2,500-calorie diet. As a triathlete, your caloric needs might be in the 3,000 to 3,500 range, and closer to 5,000 for athletes training for ultraendurance events, such as an Ironman-distance triathlon. Accordingly, nutrient requirements will be much higher.

- You might also consider using the maximum grams of fat recommended per day as a range. Thus, if you aim for a daily fat intake of 65 to 80 grams per day while increasing your recommended carbohydrate consumption, your diet will be better suited for the rigorous nutritional demands of exercise.

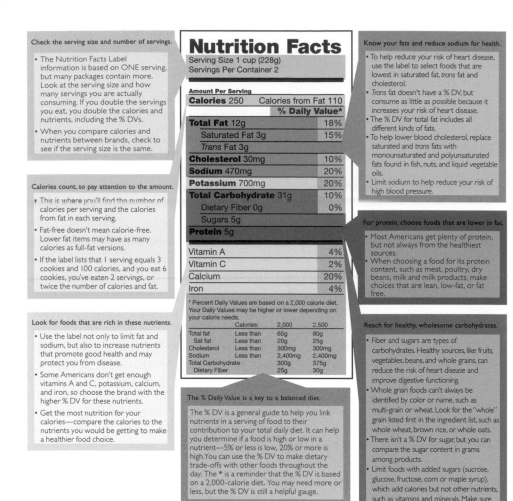

Check the serving size and number of servings.

- The Nutrition Facts Label information is based on ONE serving, but many packages contain more. Look at the serving size and how many servings you are actually consuming. If you double the servings you eat, you double the calories and nutrients, including the % DVs.
- When you compare calories and nutrients between brands, check to see if the serving size is the same.

Calories count, so pay attention to the amount.

- This is where you'll find the number of calories per serving and the calories from fat in each serving.
- Fat-free doesn't mean calorie-free. Lower fat items may have as many calories as full-fat versions.
- If the label lists that 1 serving equals 3 cookies and 100 calories, and you eat 6 cookies, you've eaten 2 servings, or twice the number of calories and fat.

Look for foods that are rich in these nutrients.

- Use the label not only to limit fat and sodium, but also to increase nutrients that promote good health and may protect you from disease.
- Some Americans don't get enough vitamins A and C, potassium, calcium, and iron, so choose the brand with the higher % DV for these nutrients.
- Get the most nutrition for your calories—compare the calories to the nutrients you would be getting to make a healthier food choice.

Know your fats and reduce sodium for health.

- To help reduce your risk of heart disease, use the label to select foods that are lowest in saturated fat, *trans* fat and cholesterol.
- *Trans* fat doesn't have a % DV, but consume as little as possible because it increases your risk of heart disease.
- The % DV for total fat includes all different kinds of fats.
- To help lower blood cholesterol, replace saturated and *trans* fats with monounsaturated and polyunsaturated fats found in fish, nuts, and liquid vegetable oils.
- Limit sodium to help reduce your risk of high blood pressure.

For protein, choose foods that are lower in fat.

- Most Americans get plenty of protein, but not always from the healthiest sources.
- When choosing a food for its protein content, such as meat, poultry, dry beans, milk and milk products, make choices that are lean, low-fat, or fat free.

Reach for healthy, wholesome carbohydrates.

- Fiber and sugars are types of carbohydrates. Healthy sources, like fruits, vegetables, beans, and whole grains, can reduce the risk of heart disease and improve digestive functioning.
- Whole grain foods can't always be identified by color or name, such as multi-grain or wheat. Look for the "whole" grain listed first in the ingredient list, such as whole wheat, brown rice, or whole oats.
- There isn't a % DV for sugar, but you can compare the sugar content in grams among products.
- Limit foods with added sugars (sucrose, glucose, fructose, corn or maple syrup), which add calories but not other nutrients, such as vitamins and minerals. Make sure that added sugars are not one of the first few items in the ingredients list.

The % Daily Value is a key to a balanced diet.

The % DV is a general guide to help you link nutrients in a serving of food to their contribution to your total daily diet. It can help you determine if a food is high or low in a nutrient—5% or less is low, 20% or more is high. You can use the % DV to make dietary trade-offs with other foods throughout the day. The * is a reminder that the % DV is based on a 2,000-calorie diet. You may need more or less, but the % DV is still a helpful gauge.

Nutrition Facts

Serving Size 1 cup (228g)
Servings Per Container 2

Amount Per Serving

Calories 250	Calories from Fat 110
	% Daily Value*
Total Fat 12g	18%
Saturated Fat 3g	15%
Trans Fat 3g	
Cholesterol 30mg	10%
Sodium 470mg	20%
Potassium 700mg	20%
Total Carbohydrate 31g	10%
Dietary Fiber 0g	0%
Sugars 5g	
Protein 5g	
Vitamin A	4%
Vitamin C	2%
Calcium	20%
Iron	4%

* Percent Daily Values are based on a 2,000 calorie diet. Your Daily Values may be higher or lower depending on your calorie needs.

	Calories:	2,000	2,500
Total fat	Less than	65g	80g
Sat fat	Less than	20g	25g
Cholesterol	Less than	300mg	300mg
Sodium	Less than	2,400mg	2,400mg
Total Carbohydrate		300g	375g
Dietary Fiber		25g	30g

Determining Your Calorie Needs

Determining how many calories you need daily as you embark on a triathlon training program can be tricky. Of course, since you'll be burning more energy on training swims, rides, and runs, your caloric needs are going to be greater. And your metabolic rate will increase with your newfound fitness, so you'll be burning more calories—even while you sleep.

How do you know how much you need to eat to keep up with your body's new caloric needs? There are several variables to consider, including body type, weight, gender, and intensity and duration of workouts.

One good rule of thumb during workouts is to increase your calories by 100 for every hour you spend in training at a low to moderate intensity level. This equates to about 30 to 60 grams of carbohydrate, which you can easily get from an energy bar or sports drink. Higher-intensity workouts (e.g., tough intervals on the track) demand even more calories, as much as 200 to 300 calories per hour.

To help determine your exact daily caloric needs for when you're not training but your body needs fuel to recover, it's best to see a sports nutritionist or dietitian.

Vitamins and Supplements

When you get involved in triathlon and start reading the magazines, you're sure to notice the plethora of magic-bullet supplements out there. They'll promise everything from increased endurance to faster times. But do they really work? Although these products might provide some performance benefits, most nutritionists agree that a healthy diet is far more beneficial to your triathlon training than anything you'll find in a pill (no matter how many advertising dollars are spent trying to convince you otherwise). Bottom line: A balanced and nutritious diet high in whole foods and complex carbohydrate is the cornerstone of good nutrition and should provide you with all the vitamins and minerals you need. However, some people take supplements to compensate for poor eating habits.

Taken to an extreme, some supplements can even harm you. Fat-soluble vitamins (A, D, E, and K) are stored in the body and can build up to toxic levels if taken in excessive amounts. If you think your diet is not quite up to par, your best bet is a multivitamin with moderate amounts of essential nutrients.

The Fluid Facts

We've touched upon the importance of fluids previously, but this is such a vital concern for triathletes that it's worth taking a closer look. Water is our most essential nutrient; we can live longer without food than we can without water. Water makes up 60 percent of body weight, and blood is 90 percent water. We need to replace lost fluids regularly throughout the day to maintain proper body temperature and energy-producing capabilities.

The body keeps cool during exercise by circulating blood to the skin, where water is lost in the form of sweat. Eventually, if you lose enough water, you'll put undue strain on your cardiovascular system, causing performance to deteriorate. In extreme cases, dehydration can lead to heart failure, among other things, and even death.

Most active people have experienced mild dehydration without knowing it. This is because the signs of mild dehydration can be subtle. To improve your performance, tune in to your body's signals of dehydration:

- Headache
- Fatigue
- Loss of appetite
- Flushed skin

- Heat intolerance
- Light-headedness
- Small amount of dark yellow urine

What You Need

An average, nonexercising adult needs about two quarts of fluids per day to replace normal water loss. Triathletes training for a multisport event obviously need more. To evaluate your fluid needs, weigh yourself before and after each workout. Every pound you lose equals approximately two cups of fluid. Drink enough fluids to compensate for any weight loss, plus your normal daily requirement of two quarts.

For particularly hard workouts on hot days, follow these guidelines:

- Before exercising, drink one to two cups of fluid.
- During exercise, drink four to six ounces of water or a sports drink every 15 to 20 minutes.
- After exercise, drink plenty of fluids right away, even if you aren't thirsty (thirst is a poor indicator of fluid needs). If your workout was particularly intense, drink more than you normally would after exercise.

ENERGY DRINKS

Energy drinks, such as Red Bull, Monster, and Rock Star, are all the rage today, especially among younger consumers. And when it comes to energy, any product that purports to provide it is inevitably going to be tied to endurance sports, whether substantiated or not.

If you've ever considered or are currently using an energy drink as a supplement to your training or racing, consider these points:

- Many energy drinks contain taurine or guarana, ingredients about which there is little existing reputable research. Most energy drinks contain some caffeine, so oftentimes the benefits of these so-called energizing ingredients are overstated.
- The scientific community has not thoroughly studied the effects of combining the ingredients in many energy drinks. Researchers don't precisely know what effect an energy drink will have on your heart rate, blood pressure, nervous system, and perception of fatigue and pain during training.
- Energy drinks can turn off your body's natural physical and mental warning flags. For example, if an energy drink revs you up so much that you feel you can go farther, faster, or harder than you should, it will cause you to push your boundaries, making you more susceptible to injury and overtraining.
- Many energy drinks are carbonated, which most endurance athletes find intolerable. During strenuous long-term aerobic exercise, carbonated beverages often lead to nausea or other stomach problems.

Types of Beverages

There are many kinds of sports nutrition products, each with its own formulation and purpose. Without knowing your needs or the products' ingredients, things can get pretty confusing.

To help clarify your choices, following are brief descriptions of the three major categories of drinks available to you today (naming brands doesn't imply endorsement—it just makes it easier to illustrate the distinctions between types). Also, new sports nutrition products are being introduced constantly, so if you don't understand their use, read the label carefully or contact the manufacturer. At the end of this chapter, you'll find a usage chart that sums up your sports nutrition choices.

Sports Drinks

Sports drinks help replace fluids, carbohydrate, electrolytes, and vital nutrients lost during exercise. Usually, these drinks are somewhat sweet, from mild to strong, depending on the brand and flavor. They contain glucose, fructose, or a glucose polymer or, in many cases, a combination of these ingredients as a carbohydrate source. They might also contain nutrients, such as potassium and sodium, which are depleted during exercise. Brands include Gatorade, Powerade, Cytomax, and Hydra Fuel.

Carbo-Loading and Recovery Drinks

These beverages are for use before or after exercise or as a carbohydrate supplement. They typically contain a carbohydrate source similar to that of their sports drink counterparts, but they have more of it. For example, although the carbohydrate potency of most sports drinks falls in the 6 to 8 percent range, carbo-loading and recovery drinks can have 20 percent or more carbohydrate.

So does that mean more carbohydrate is better, and that, because this stuff is stronger, you should be using it during exercise? In this case, more is definitely not better. During exercise, you need something that will digest easily and be absorbed quickly into your bloodstream. Researchers have found that a 6 to 8 percent carbohydrate solution works best to accomplish this during exercise. The high carbohydrate content of recovery drinks will help you recover faster from the workout, and the stronger solution shouldn't upset your stomach when you are not exercising. Brands include Gatorade Protein Recovery, CytoMax Recovery, and Ultra Fuel.

Balanced Nutrition Shakes

Sometimes referred to as sports shakes, these drinks are typically dairy or dairy-like and include vital nutrients without the bulk. They contain mostly carbohydrate, a moderate amount of protein, and a small amount of fat and are often packed with vitamins and minerals. Several products are even lactose-free, reducing the risk of nausea in lactose-intolerant athletes. Balanced nutrition shakes are great for people who have a hard time eating well. The shakes make a quick, healthy snack, preevent meal, or recovery drink. Brands include Gatorade Sports Nutrition Shake and Balance. In the mainstream market, products such as Ensure and Boost are similar.

CHOOSING A BEVERAGE

You now know that sports drinks can supply you with vital fluids, carbohydrate for energy, and vital nutrients such as sodium and potassium. But out of all the available brands, how do you choose the one that's right for you? These tips might help:

- Avoid carbonated drinks; these can cause gastrointestinal distress. This distress, in turn, will likely cause you to drink less fluid, which can lead to dehydration.
- Avoid beverages containing alcohol or caffeine. They are diuretics and contribute to fluid loss.
- Choose a drink that tastes good. If it doesn't have a pleasant taste, you're not likely to drink enough of it.
- Choose a drink with a carbohydrate concentration of 6 to 8 percent. Studies have shown that this is the optimal range because it is absorbed from the intestine significantly faster than anything over an 8 percent concentration, and it is absorbed 30 percent faster than water.

Your Sports Nutrition Choices

The following chart might help clarify some of the product choices triathletes have. As you'll see, there is a lot of crossover usage between products. For example, a sports drink, such as Gatorade, is primarily designed for use during exercise, but there's certainly no harm in having some before exercise, after exercise, or at anytime during the day. An energy bar is good just about anytime as well, but don't eat it during a race unless you've tested it for digestibility under training conditions.

The circled checkmarks in the chart denote the product's primary uses; the others represent secondary uses. If an area is not marked, the product is not appropriate for this purpose. Also, remember that a "Before" designation means that you should consume these products one to two hours before exercise to allow for digestion.

Sports Nutrition Product Usage

	Before exercise	During exercise	After exercise	Anytime
Sports drinks	✓	✔	✓	✓
Carbohydrate loading/recovery drinks	✔		✔	✓
Balanced nutrition shakes	✔		✔	✔
Energy bars	✔	✓	✔	✔
Carbohydrate gels	✓	✔	✓	✓

Note: For training and racing longer than the Olympic distance, energy bars can be used during exercise.

✔ = Primary use

✓ = Secondary use

chapter 9

Staying Healthy

Health is our natural state.

—Deepak Chopra

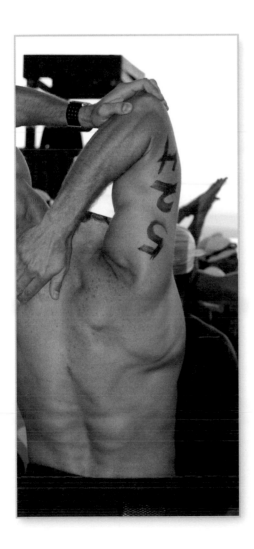

In the late 1970s, when thousands took to running marathons, many of these enthusiastic runners didn't train properly, and soon they were plagued with overuse and trauma injuries. To add insult to injury (literally), few in the traditional medical community had expertise in sports medicine. So if you went to your doctor, he or she would have probably told you to stop running. (The late Dr. George Sheehan said, "The jogger has three natural enemies: drivers, dogs, and doctors.")

Many triathletes come from running backgrounds, and you might have your own tales of injury battles won and lost. You probably know that cross-training lowers your susceptibility to injury, and perhaps that's one of the factors that helped you decide to jump into multisports.

Sports injuries are most often caused by overuse. A key word to remember here is *moderation*. Moderation comes from the Latin word *moderatus*, which mean to limit extremes. The focus of the first part of this chapter is steering clear of injuries and the overtraining that leads to them. And for those who are currently injured (or sustain an injury in the future), I've provided an overview of the six injuries most common to triathletes, as well as some recovery, training adjustment, and prevention tips.

Preventing Injuries

Although fitness and health might seem synonymous, many marathoners have ruined their knees by putting in too much distance in too little time. Sure, their heart rates might be phenomenal—maybe 40 or 44 beats per minute, which indicates a strong, efficient cardiovascular system. But they're hobbling around because they sacrificed their health in an effort to attain fitness.

"Most triathletes are not pros. They participate as part of a lifestyle," says Dr. Daryll Hobson, a physician who has treated several professional triathletes, including Mark Allen. "They enter the sport with the idea that 'if I'm fit, I'm going to be healthy,' which is a mistake. In striving for fitness, they often destroy their health. Many triathletes tend to want to get someplace very quickly, too. They're not willing to do the work of establishing a high level of fitness performance and maintaining health simultaneously."

Importance of Rest

It might sound simplistic, but you can avoid most injuries by building enough rest into a training program. As you learned in the chapters on training, rest is crucial to any good triathlon regimen. Yet rest is perhaps the hardest thing for a competitive triathlete to do. One look at the number of articles and books written on sports injuries clearly shows that athletes and physically active people have a hard time resting.

Runners are particularly notorious for overdoing it. In *The Runner's Complete Medical Guide* (Mangi et al. 1979), the authors address the irony of running injuries: "Runners are the fittest group of sick and injured people in the world. While running is probably the most natural and healthful sport ever played, its participants most frequently push their mental and physical capacities to the limit."

Most sports injuries result from not allowing the body enough rest and recovery time. Planning and following a smart and effective training schedule that builds in rest days and easy training days for recovery is crucial to avoiding injury. But even if you do that, there's still a possibility that you need a long period of rest, especially if you've gone berserk and have been training hard and racing just about every weekend (not uncommon for overzealous newcomers to the sport).

Forcing yourself to take a long rest is particularly important if you've been training for and just completed a full triathlon season in an area that features good weather year-round and holds plenty of multisport events within driving distance. In many subtle ways, the long months of training have taken their toll on your body and maybe on your mind. (Can you spell B-U-R-N-O-U-T?)

Balance and Belief: The Key to Success

Larry Rosa

In just his third triathlon, Chris Lieto found himself running his first marathon during the final leg of the Hawaiian Ironman in 1998. Barely a year earlier, he was inspired to take up the sport after he watched the Ironman on television, befriended professional triathlete Wendy Ingram, and read an inspiring article by the legendary Mark Allen.

Although he obviously discovered some natural endurance, Chris attributes his early and fast success to the muscle between his ears: "I believed in myself, that not only could I just finish, but I could do well in my first Ironman, even though it was just my third race," says Chris. "I think that's a lesson for everyone, especially the newcomer. You first have to believe that you can finish a triathlon. You see it in your mind; you start believing it and accepting it."

The professional triathlete is a resident of Danville, California, and is a three-time Ironman champion and former U.S. national Ironman champion. Year after year Chris' discipline and dedication to the sport of triathlon have paid off.

In addition to training and racing, Chris has always made it a top priority to have balance in his work and family life. "If you have family and a vocation you're passionate about, you have to stay balanced while you're training and racing. It's about a healthy lifestyle, so it's important not to sacrifice family when you get involved in sport," Chris advised.

And, although Chris works hard in triathlon, he's a big believer in working smarter, taking time to recover, and not overdoing it. "Success in triathlon is about putting in a reasonable amount of training time for the distance you're aiming for, not putting in an ungodly amount of hours. I train less now than I did five years ago because I know now that balance is more important. Sometimes recovery time is more crucial for success than training time."

The problem is that many triathletes are bundles of nervous energy. Triathlon can become an addiction, albeit a healthy one. Without the soothing effect of the exercise high, many triathletes find it difficult to take a rest day or build an easy swim, bike ride, or run workout into a training schedule.

Listening to Your Body

Just how do you know when to take an easy day or maybe even a day or two off from training altogether? World-class athletes learn to monitor their internal workings, to be in tune with any—however slight—indication of pending injury. When professional endurance athletes feel they are pushing that fine line between greater performance and injury, the wiser ones know to back off.

Endurance training makes the constant monitoring of bodily processes a necessity. "Listen to your body" becomes a divine commandment when applied to training. Injury is the price paid for disobedience. Most experts concur that athletes who have greater body awareness are more likely to avoid overtraining. Yet, with all the internal variables (not to mention external variables such as bike fit, technique, and equipment), how can you go about establishing a body awareness as keen as that of a trained professional? How do you know when you're pushing that human stress gauge to the maximum?

When Training Leads to Unhealthy Stress

When you train, a certain amount of stress is normal. But once you begin to overtrain, unhealthy stress and the symptoms that go along with it often precede injury. Perhaps the best opportunity to monitor your stress level is the sympathetic nervous system. This system mediates the response of the body to stress, playing a major role in speeding up heart rate, increasing blood pressure, and mobilizing energy reserves. Forty years of research by stress researcher and renowned expert Hans Selye on the sympathetic nervous system shows that there is a point in the human body when a healthy stress level can become unhealthy stress. Dr. Hobson, a big believer in Hans Selye's research, contends that there are signs of an overstressed body. View the signs as the body's natural gauge with a well-defined red line (Mora 1991).

Possible Signs of Overtraining

Although these symptoms are general warnings of possible injuries, your own experience will teach you the specific signs that tell you you're training too hard. The warning signs that can foretell pending injury for one person might be false alarms for others. For example, I often experience sugar cravings, eye strain, and moodiness when I overtrain, but I rarely have the other symptoms listed here:

- A strong craving for sugar on rest days
- Inconsistent episodes of blurred vision and a feeling of eye strain and sensitivity
- Varying degrees of joint pain, particularly in the vulnerable sacroiliac (lower back) and knee
- Muscle weakness, particularly in the calf and medial (inner) side of the knee
- Getting sick easily with slow recovery
- Allergic reactions (more than usual)
- Insomnia or an inability to relax and subsequent loss of sleep
- Poor digestion
- Excessive nervousness and irritability
- Lack of energy with no reserve energy to surge in the latter half of a workout
- Episodes of dizziness when standing up from a lying or squatting position
- Increased or racing heart rate

Tips on Getting Back to Health

If you're currently in the throes of overtraining, here are some concrete steps you can take to get back on track:

- **Get reacquainted.** There are only so many hours in the day, and if you're like many triathletes trying to make a living and train too, swimming, biking, and running take up a large portion of your free time. If, as a result, you haven't stayed in touch with family or friends, now is the perfect time to make it up to them.

- **Catch up on sleep.** Has your training schedule wreaked havoc with your sleeping pattern? Do you get up an hour earlier to get in that run during the week before going to work? Sleep deprivation is cumulative; if you've found your body slow to recover from long or hard runs, the cause could be months of not getting enough sleep. Give yourself a break and allow yourself the proper amount of sleep (whatever that may be—it's different for everyone).

- **Get away from it all.** One of the best ways to recover is to plan a getaway. You don't have to take a week off; even a weekend trip within driving distance can do wonders to rejuvenate your body and mind.

- **Get a massage.** If you can't afford the time or cost of a weekend vacation, try a nice, relaxing massage. The right kind of massage can speed the recovery process, especially for overuse injuries. It helps improve the blood supply to muscles, improves circulation, and speeds healing.

- **Cut your mileage.** If you just can't bear to be away from running, at least cut your mileage significantly for a few weeks or even months. If you've been doing speedwork, such as intervals on the track, give your body a break from these difficult workouts. If you've been doing hard hill workouts, cut down or eliminate those from your program as well.

Stretching for Health

As a whole, we triathletes tend to be a tightly muscled group. If we aren't grabbing our Achilles tendons in pain, we're probably massaging our aching hamstrings from yesterday's track workout. Ironically, we tend to be a lazy group when it comes to stretching.

Yet stretching is one of the simplest ways to increase fitness, enhance the quality of your life, and improve athletic performance. Anybody can do it, and it doesn't require any further financial resources or a great degree of energy. That's not to say you don't have to work at it; you do. But the long-term rewards outweigh the initial investment.

If you've never been a fan of stretching, either before or after exercise, prepare to commit to this activity on a new level. Stretching takes patience, but it can improve your performances.

> ## *RACING TIP*
>
> The goal on race day is not just to complete your event but to be fit *and* healthy when you cross the finish line. If you've properly trained and tapered, you should feel fresh and energetic, with no muscle aches or soreness. During a race, don't throw your careful attention to health out the window. Listen to your body and heed warning signs indicating that you're pushing too hard. Don't be afraid to seek medical attention on the race course if you feel severe pain, dizziness, or are debilitated in any way.

You might think of flexibility training as arduous and time consuming. Two reasons many athletes have a poor or nonexistent stretching program are it's not a competitive activity and it's hard to measure progress. Flexibility training is so passive that, ultimately, the primary motivation must come from a firm commitment to a balanced program, with a long-term vision of the benefits.

Not only do you have to be committed, you have to be consistent with your stretching program. If you begin a program, see some improvement, and then abandon your stretching for months, your body will regress back to its previous range of motion, thus negating all the effort and time you've put in.

Flexibility can help you increase your fitness level in a foundational way that affects almost every aspect of your exercise program. With flexibility, you can safely train for cardiovascular fitness, strength, and speed. Without flexibility, your range of motion in almost any activity is limited, and you become much more susceptible to injury.

Visualize that a normal running muscle is 5 inches (13 cm) long. When lactate builds up in the muscle (like during a strenuous run or during the latter stages of a marathon), the muscle shortens to 3 inches (8 cm). But if you can improve your running stride by half an inch (about 1 cm), the impact on your time will astound you. It can improve your marathon by minutes.

For swimming, increases in range of motion can have similarly dramatic results. If you increase your range of motion in your trunk rotation, for example, your stroke will improve. If your trunk rotation is a little better, your roll in the water is better, and thus your reach is going to help you go a little farther with each stroke. Even if you improve your trunk rotation minimally, the effect can be great. It can add up to an inch per stroke, and when you apply that to a kilometer of swimming, it can take minutes off your best swimming time.

More Stretching Benefits

If you're like me, you'd rather just jump into your running shoes and head out on the trails before the sun goes down. Let's admit it: Stretching isn't the most exciting thing to do. But a quick review of the benefits derived from greater flexibility might help you look at stretching in a new way:

- **Improved performance.** I've already discussed how stretching has a positive impact on your running and swimming; the most attractive benefit of stretching for the triathlete is the improved physical performance. The more flexible a joint, the better it can move through a bigger range of motion and thus function more efficiently. Research at the Human Performance Laboratory at Boise State University showed that 20 minutes of stretching three times a week can increase range of motion by 30 percent.

  More specifically, stretching improves the ability of muscle fibers to generate force despite lactic acid accumulation. Because muscle fibers act by contracting, the longer they are to begin with, the more they are able to contract. You achieve optimal flexibility when your normal muscle fibers are as long as possible; then, when they do inevitably shorten with lactic acid accumulation, as during prolonged exercise, they are still able to function efficiently.

- **Injury prevention.** Exercise physiologists generally agree that greater flexibility and, hence, greater range of motion, makes a person less likely to become injured. Also, stretching before your main workout warms muscles and introduces your body to the workout more gradually so that the possibility of injuries from working cold muscles too hard without a proper warm-up is decreased. However, know that cold muscles are less elastic, making them less capable of moving through a full range of motion, which can lead to strains or tears. So stretch *after* you warm your muscles through mild exercise first.

- **Improved coordination.** Greater flexibility increases neuromuscular coordination. It has been shown that the speed of nerve impulses is enhanced with stretching. The central nervous system becomes more sensitive to the physical demands placed on it, so opposing muscle groups work in a more coordinated way.

- **Greater joint elasticity.** Stretching increases tissue temperature, which in turn increases the blood supply and nutrients to the joint structure. This process promotes greater elasticity in the surrounding tissue, which makes the entire joint mechanism work more fluidly together, ensuring better and safer movement.

- **Better posture and movement.** Stretching improves muscular balance and awareness. It helps to realign soft tissue structures, which might have developed poorly through a lifetime of poor posture or normal wear and tear. Realigning tissue structures helps promote and maintain good posture, healthy movement in daily activities, and better form in running.

- **Decreased back pain.** Incidents of lower-back pain decrease for those who stretch regularly. The American Council on Exercise finds strong clinical evidence that lumbar-pelvic flexibility, including hamstrings, hip flexors, and muscles attached to the pelvis, is critical in decreasing stress to the lumbar spine.

- **Relieved muscle tension.** Stretching can relieve muscle tension. When muscles are tense for a long time (as in during long endurance running), the flow of oxygen to these muscles can be cut off. The result is a buildup of lactic acid in tissues, causing fatigue and muscle tightness or knotting. Stretching can help break up those muscle knots and release lactic acid into the bloodstream.

The Stretching Question

If you've read running books and subscribed to *Runner's World* or any other running publication, chances are you've come across a lot of material on stretching. There are about as many stretching techniques and exercises for runners and triathletes as there are sports drinks. The optimal stretching technique has always been—and will probably always be—a matter of controversy.

However, the technique most sports therapists recommend is static stretching. This conservative technique, traditionally accepted as safe and effective, involves slow elongation through a full range of motion to a point of slight discomfort. This type of stretching produces long-term gains that are maintained in people who practice it consistently. Static stretching is of low intensity and imposes less microtrauma to the tissue, resulting in better flexibility without the risk that exists with more radical (and painful) stretching techniques.

Specific stretching instructions and illustrations are beyond the scope of this book, but you can find plenty of stretching exercises with photos online or in triathlon magazines. To give you a start, here are a few areas to focus on and why they're important.

- **Shoulder and upper back.** Swimming and, to some degree, cycling, add stress and strain in this area, so it's best to keep things flexible with frequent stretching.
- **Upper leg and hamstrings.** Many lower-back injures stem from tight hamstrings, so it's important to focus on this major muscle.
- **Quadriceps.** Running and cycling, in particular, put a wallop on your quads, so be sure to stretch them out, particularly after a long or intense ride or run.
- **Triceps.** You'll be putting a lot of stress on your triceps in the pool, so make sure you integrate some stretching for this key set of swimming muscles.
- **Groin and hip.** Keeping your core flexible is just as important as keeping it strong. Make sure you stretch these areas, particularly after a long ride or run.
- **Back.** Sitting hunched over on your bicycle's aerobars can cause back problems. Besides trying to stretch out your back while riding (while you're coasting, of course), keep your back supple with plenty of stretches.

In addition to static stretching, Pilates and yoga are excellent ways of stretching as well as strengthening and balancing your body, which can also help prevent injury. Although these alternative activities are more akin to dynamic stretching, where you move through the stretching motion (rather than hold it), when done properly, they are safe and can make you a more flexible, injury-free triathlete.

Taking Care of Your Feet

By far, running causes the most injuries to triathletes. Of all the things that you can do to prevent running injuries, caring for your feet is the most crucial. Your poor feet take the brunt of the pounding as they propel you over unforgiving surfaces. The fact that these 52 oddly shaped bones, crunched inside a couple of little skin bags, can handle all that stress is rather remarkable.

If you've been running for some time, you've probably already had your share of foot pains. Perhaps they've been caused by something as simple as wearing socks that are either too thick or too loose. (Wearing properly fitted socks will prevent bunching or looseness in your shoes, which often leads to blisters or irritation.) Maybe you rushed through your running shoe purchase or received bad advice from a salesperson and are running in the wrong shoes. No matter how your foot woes originated, avoiding most problems takes just a little effort. Whether foot problems are a commonplace occurrence or a rarity for you, you can avoid most conditions with some TLC and common sense, not only in the running store, but at home and on the road. The following foot care tips are provided by Dr. George Tsatsos, a sports physician with a specialty in podiatry:

- Avoid irregular terrain, such as areas of mud and sand, or poorly maintained trails.
- Wear socks that wick away moisture, such as polypropelene or wool.
- Change your socks twice a day.
- If you have two pairs of running shoes, alternate the two so that one is always drying. This will decrease the possibility of athlete's foot.
- Use an antifungal powder. Make sure you cover the areas between the toes.

Also, if you do happen to get a blister and it hasn't burst, make a small hole at the edge with a sterilized pin or needle. Drain the fluid but leave as much of the skin as possible covering the wound. Clean and sterilize the blister and cover the wound with a second skin or blister plaster. You can tape it if it's particularly painful.

Six Injuries Most Common to Triathletes (and How to Avoid Them)

Hopefully, you're too new to the sport to have experienced serious injury. The best way to avoid any of the following common injuries is to be aware of them and to respond appropriately when you feel them coming on. But just in case you have already gotten yourself in a mess, I'll cover some recovery tips, as well as training adjustments you can make. I've talked to several experts in the field of sports medicine, but no chapter in a book can replace a proper diagnosis and the expert treatment and advice you'll get from a physician specializing in sports injuries. With that in mind, let's start from the top.

Rotator Cuff Tendinitis (or Tear)

Swimmer's shoulder is a general term often used to describe many types of shoulder problems, including muscle strains, pulls, and tendinitis. Rotator cuff tendinitis is frequently caused by pool workouts that are either too long or too hard, an imbalance in shoulder muscles, or poor stroke form. Inflammation occurs because of microscopic muscle tears and stress on the four major shoulder muscles that run together, known as the rotator cuff. Pain is usually localized (confined to that area), though it might radiate down the arm. Stiffness and difficulty extending your arm at a 90-degree angle, weakness when lifting the arm, and pain at night are indications of rotator cuff tendinitis.

Recovery

For minor cases, rest, ice, and compression of the shoulder with an elastic wrap will help reduce pain. Rest for at least a week, maybe more depending on the level of pain and soreness. Don't resume training until you can move without any pain. In severe cases, an orthopedic surgeon might recommend arthroscopic surgery.

Training Adjustments

Unfortunately, the healing process for this injury is slow because of the poor blood supply in the area. Repetitive activities that cause you to extend your arm will increase the inflammation and the risk of a tear. Therefore, unless your case is minor, your sports physician will probably want you to put any swimming or upper-body weight training workouts on hold until the shoulder is healthy. Depending on your position, you might aggravate the injury on a bicycle. Sitting upright on a stationary or indoor bicycle machine without taking your shoulder to a 90-degree angle is a good alternative exercise.

Prevention Tips

Don't increase your distance or interval workout in the pool too quickly. Work on developing balanced strength in your shoulders by weight training of your biceps, deltoids, pectorals, and trapezius muscles.

SI Dysfunction (Lower-Back Pain)

The sacroiliac (SI) joint is a major joint in the body connecting the back and the hip. Unlike other joints surrounded by muscle, the SI relies predominantly on ligaments for support. When these ligaments become irritated, either by a structural or muscle imbalance, the term *SI dysfunction* is often used to describe this sports injury. The pain is usually located in the lower-back area, just above the hip, and is a dull ache, but it can become sharp if training continues. Sometimes the pain radiates to other areas of the back and hip.

"I prefer to use the term pelvic twist," says Dr. P. Michael Leahy, advisor to the American Chiropractic Association's Council on Sports Injury and Physical Fitness. "The SI is not the only thing involved. You have to look at muscle weakness or structural problems; sometimes it's both." Several years ago, Dr. Leahy compiled statistics on common injuries to triathletes at the Ironman Triathlon in Hawaii. He found SI dysfunction to be one of the three injuries most common to multisport athletes.

Recovery

Because of the poor blood supply to ligaments in the lower back, the road to complete recovery can take some time, but Leahy estimates that one-third of lower-back injuries can be attributed to structural imbalances, thus requiring relatively simple treatment. Studies have shown that chiropractic manipulation, in conjunction with back stretching and strengthening exercises, can be very effective.

Training Adjustments

Lower-back problems can occur in and be affected by many sports, which makes any training extremely difficult. If your case is mild and is not aggravated by swimming, your sports physician might allow some low-level workouts. Once the pain has subsided and your doctor gives you the green light, gradually work your way back to your normal routine.

Prevention Tips

Locate and correct any structural imbalances in your running or cycling motion (such as those caused by a difference in leg length). A certified sports medicine physician can help you locate imbalances and suggest ways to correct them or limit their impact on you. Check your aero position on the bicycle—is it uncomfortable and causing you back pain? If so, better to sacrifice a little aerodynamics for greater comfort and health. Also, identify and strengthen any weak muscles that might cause lower-back problems. By implementing a lower-back stretching and strengthening regimen when you're healthy, you'll avoid most back problems. You might also consider taking a Pilates class with a focus on core training. It will help you build up your core and establish good balance and posture.

Hamstring Muscle Tear

A hamstring muscle tear might occur suddenly while you are running or cycling, particularly during an intense session, such as an interval workout or a finish-line sprint. Downhill running is another possible cause. The tear is usually caused by tight hamstrings, often due to overtraining or muscle imbalance. Hamstring muscle tears often occur at the tendons near the knee or hip, though a tear in the central portion of the hamstring is not uncommon. The pain is usually sharp and located in a very specific area. Muscle spasms can occur as well.

"Hamstring problems can be very persistent; you may think you have it licked, and it comes back," says Lisa Alamar, certified structural therapist who has worked with many professional athletes in her Oak Park, Illinois, office. "Recurring hamstring problems usually stem from a muscle or structural imbalance between the hamstrings and muscles in the thigh and buttock region."

Recovery

With a mild case, a day off with gentle stretching and massage should make the pain go away. If it persists, use ice and an anti-inflammatory pain reliever such as aspirin or ibuprofen, and elevate the legs to help decrease the inflammation. An elastic wrap will help reduce the pull on the inflamed area. Many sports medicine physicians recommend heat after a few days to improve circulation in the area.

Training Adjustments

Depending on the severity of the tear, some light running might be approved by your sports physician 48 hours after the injury. When you return to running, go easy on the hamstrings by taking short strides and avoiding downhill running or banked tracks. Water running is an excellent alternative exercise to reduce the strain on the hamstrings.

Prevention Tips

Hamstrings are generally weaker than quadriceps. Most sports physicians recommend hamstring curls and other strength training exercises that will give you better muscle balance. (Hamstrings should be at least 60 percent as strong as the quadriceps.) Frequent stretching of the hamstrings is also beneficial. You might consider adding a rowing machine routine to your training; this is not only excellent endurance training, but strengthens your hamstrings, lower back, abs, and quadriceps.

Iliotibial Band Syndrome

The iliotibial band is located on the outer side of the leg, from the hip to the knee. Common to both runners and cyclists, iliotibial band syndrome is an inflammation caused by the iliotibial band tendons rubbing against the outer bone of the knee. The pain is usually located on the outside portion of the knee, but irritation can occur anywhere between the knee and the buttocks. Though the pain is not disabling, unless corrected, this injury can persistently ruin your workouts.

"Iliotibial band syndrome is a relatively minor injury that should be treated by solving any mechanical problems, calming the muscle, increasing flexibility, and improving strength," says Robert P. Nirschl, orthopedic surgeon, and medical director of the Virginia Sports Medicine Institute. In cases where the injury is relatively minor, massage can also help.

Recovery

If your injury is due to a structural imbalance, orthotics might be all you need. (These are shoe insoles that replace the generic ones that come with shoes. The best orthotics are custom-built by a sports podiatrist to support your unique feet.) If iliotibial band syndrome is caused by overuse, you simply need to decrease the intensity for a week or two. Icing the area and taking aspirin or ibuprofen can help reduce inflammation.

Training Adjustments

Try water running or light cycling. Avoid high-intensity workouts until the injury is healed. This includes hills or any type of varying terrain that can cause the injury to reoccur.

Prevention Tips

Implement a regular stretching and strengthening program, with particular emphasis on the outer thigh and knee muscles. Also, don't run in worn-out shoes; the wear on the outside of the heel can cause this nagging malady.

Achilles Tendinitis

Located at the back of the ankle at the junction where the large calf muscles attach to the heel bone, the Achilles tendon is vulnerable to microscopic tears and inflammation from the repetitive motion of running. Achilles tendinitis can be caused by overpronation or by the shortening of the calves brought on by excessive hill running or overtraining. The pain is localized with general tightness in the ankle area. Another sure sign is intense pain when walking on the balls of your feet or your toes.

"It's very common for a runner never to give an injured Achilles tendon a good chance to get healthy," says Boulder sports physician Dr. Hobson. "And if the injury has progressed, the surrounding tissue becomes inflamed, creating a situation where . . . the chances of the injury recurring are high."

Stretching your Achilles tendons between sections of the race will help you avoid cramping and injury.

Recovery

Icing the area will reduce the inflammation. For support, wrap the ankle with elastic bandage or tape (though your main support should be a good running shoe with a stable heel). Some sports physicians recommend moist (never dry) heat before and after low-intensity exercise to help loosen muscles and bring more blood to the area. Orthotics or an elevated heel are often recommended to control overpronation.

Training Adjustments

The Achilles tendon is yet another slow healer due to poor blood supply. If your sports physician considers the Achilles tendinitis to be a minor case and if it is caught early enough, he or she might allow low-intensity, light running.

Prevention Tips

Use a good pair of running shoes with a stable heel, and watch for wear along the outer edges of the heel. Avoid steep hill climbing and running on hard surfaces. Stretch the Achilles tendon, calf, and hamstring muscles before and after you run. The best prevention is strength training for all the lower leg muscles, a vulnerable part of the body that is subject to high stress from running.

Plantar Fasciitis (Heel Pain)

The plantar fascia is a ligament that runs through the arch of the foot. Each time you plant your foot, your body's weight is distributed throughout the foot and the fascia is stretched. Plantar fasciitis is caused by overtraining, foot imbalances, running on hard surfaces, or running in worn-out shoes. All of these things can overstretch and strain the ligament, resulting in tiny tears and inflammation. The pain and area of tenderness is located underneath the foot, at the front of the heel. Usually, the onset of pain is gradual, but increases with continued running. A common symptom of plantar fasciitis is intense pain when awakening in the morning, especially with the first few steps.

Recovery

Plantar fasciitis is considered a serious running injury; if it's not treated properly, further tearing could cause severe damage and take several months to heal. Consult a sports podiatrist for expert treatment. (He or she will most likely recommend the use of orthotics.) Self-therapy should include ice and aspirin or ibuprofen to relieve inflammation.

Training Adjustments

In severe cases, though it might be a tough prescription to swallow, any activity that puts pressure on your foot is not recommended. (Swimming, preferably with a pull buoy, is a good alternative.) In mild cases, most sports physicians will allow light running.

Prevention Tips

Many running coaches recommend the use of orthotics even if you don't have any foot problems. Also, stretch the plantar fascia. Avoid running on hard surfaces, and don't run in worn-out shoes that have little or no cushioning.

chapter 10

Peaking to Race

Your progress toward success depends on a fundamental question: Where are you going?

—Napoleon Hill

George Sheehan said, "The race, where I can be a hero, is a contest where I give my word of honor to go out and do battle with myself." He's right. The race is today's equivalent of a battlefield. But instead of fighting an opponent, we battle ourselves with every stroke, pedal, and stride. Whether they be triathlons, running races, or cycling time trials, races are personal arenas for heroism. Whatever your race goal, you owe it to yourself to have a good race. The key to having a good race is proper training first and then making sure you cover all those little details.

Details, Details

Don't fall into the preevent bloopers that these guys do:

- The careless triathlete who trains for six months or more to compete in a sprint-distance triathlon, only to experience stomach pains during a race from eating a superburrito supreme just minutes before the start.

- The mechanically challenged (you know who you are) who don't check the air pressure in their tires, only to find themselves riding on their rims through the transition area.

- The type A who can't resist putting in one last hard run the day before the big race, only to find that she doesn't have fresh legs when she gets on the bike (duh).

Isn't it ironic that some people train so long and hard, only to sabotage their efforts by paying little or no attention to some small (but definitely not minor) details that can dramatically affect the outcome of a race? The last thing you want to do after putting in all that work is to blow it by botching a little thing like the wrong meal before a race, failing to tend to a mechanical problem, or a poorly timed hard workout. In the weeks before an event, it's the little things, the small details, that count.

Sweating the details doesn't just help you avoid disaster. It can help you be more mentally and physically prepared to have a great race. By tending to all the details we'll focus on in this chapter, you'll feel more confident, better prepared, and ready to peak for the big event.

What to Do in the Weeks Before a Race

First things first: Congratulate yourself. You are a few weeks away from what might be one of the most rewarding efforts you'll make in your life. You've made it this far, and you're still standing (hopefully). Training for a triathlon, even for a sprint distance, is no small task. It takes commitment, self-discipline, and an unfaltering capacity for bearing with aches and pains.

You've made it through the scorching hot and humid summer runs when garden sprinklers were few and far between. You've weathered the chilly spring mornings on your bike, when you wished your helmet had a heater. You've tolerated inconsiderate toddlers invading your lap swimming lane. You've come a long way and are probably in better shape than 99 percent of the population. Take pride in your accomplishment. You're ready to complete your first triathlon, up the distance, or go for a personal best. Whatever your goal, congratulate yourself on just getting to where you are now.

But don't pat yourself on the back for too long. You've still got a few weeks to go. Even if your training hasn't been perfect or you've overtrained a little, the next few weeks are the critical zone, a period where it's essential that you pay attention to some vital details.

Complete Your Last Long Run

Running takes the greatest toll on your body, so make sure you give yourself plenty of time to recover before your race. You should do your last long run, but not your longest, approximately 14 days before the race. Run a distance roughly equivalent to half of your longest previous run. Some triathletes run their longest run on this day, but elite runners have ideal muscle composition for running (predominantly slow-twitch fibers) that allow for quick recovery. The majority of triathletes require more time, so your longest run should be three to four weeks before race day.

Stick to the Tapering Schedule You've Set for Yourself

If you've been following the training advice in part II, tapering will already be built into your training calendar. Triathletes often find this phase of training the most mentally difficult to deal with. The thinking usually goes something like this: "I've been training hard. My body has adapted well. I'm in great shape for the big race. Why in the world would I want to let up?"

Believe it or not, if you've trained as hard as you think you have, your body has to recover from the cumulative distance you've put on your feet, legs, and arms. Although you might feel just fine, there are likely microscopic tears in your muscle tissue, tears that need a few weeks of easy training and a few rest days to completely heal.

If you have any doubts about the value of tapering and are itching to just ditch this part of your training plan, consider a little scientific evidence. A study at Malaspina College in British Columbia and the University of Alberta shows how necessary tapering is to triathletes. In the study, 25 athletes trained for an hour five days a week for six weeks at a high-intensity level of 75 to 85 percent (Mora 1993). After six weeks, seven athletes tapered for three days, cutting down on volume (not intensity), and a second group tapered for six days. A third group tapered by doing no exercise at all for four full days, and an unfortunate bunch in the fourth group exercised at the same intensity and volume until test day (equivalent to race day).

The results showed a 12 percent increase of the lactate threshold level in both the three-day and six-day taper groups. (For the purposes of this study, the lactate threshold is a measure of how long the athletes could maintain a certain exercise intensity before too much lactic acid, a waste byproduct of exercise, builds in the blood.) The no-exercise group made no improvement, and the train-to-death group *decreased* their lactate threshold level.

Glycogen levels were also measured. (Remember, your glycogen storage is like a fuel tank; the more glycogen you have, the longer you can go.) Glycogen storage levels soared by 25 percent with the six-day program. The three-day and the no-exercise groups showed an increase of 12 percent. Once again, the train-to-death group smelled of overtraining: Their glycogen levels *dropped* 12 percent.

"My focus was the cellular level, finding the physiological results of tapering. Of course, everybody wants to know about performance," says J.P. Neary, PhD, who headed the study. "The results determine that a little extra rest helps cells work more efficiently during exercise."

Neary emphasizes that tapering is subject to a host of variables specific to the individual and the training event. For example, a half-Ironman distance race requires longer, slower training than used in the study, and older athletes tend to require longer recovery times. Thus triathletes training for longer distances might do better with more tapering; older triathletes might also need more tapering. The point is to stick to the tapering suggestions and sample tapering charts presented in chapter 7. Don't let the excitement of the pending drama or your impatience ruin your chances of having a great race.

Watch Your Diet

There are a few important areas to consider concerning your diet in the weeks preceding the big event:

- If you've been following the recommended 65 to 70 percent carbohydrate diet for a triathlete, your pantry should be well-stocked with pasta, grains, fruits, and vegetables. (If not, do some shopping.)

- Are you staying away from high-fat foods like cheese, whole milk, and butter? Make an effort to fine-tune your diet. If you haven't been a good boy or girl, make a commitment to get your nutritional act together in the coming critical weeks. You've come too far to let diet stop you from being your very best. The key word here is fine-tune. Don't make any last-minute drastic diet changes that will be hard on your body.

- If you have a deficiency of protein in your diet, integrate some legumes, egg whites, and low-fat dairy products into your diet.

- Are you keeping well hydrated? Make sure you drink 6 to 10 eight-ounce (240 mL) glasses of water a day.

Try Some Mental Training

You've come far in your physical training, but have you trained your mind with positive thoughts and visualization of the finish line? If not, devote some time to this important, but often overlooked, detail.

Begin to set aside 15 to 30 minutes every day in a quiet place where you won't be interrupted. Close your eyes and relax. Take deep, slow breaths, inhaling through your mouth and exhaling through your nose. Visualize every phase of the race, from starting line to the glorious finish. See yourself relaxed and confident on the day of the race. You're calm and cool within the hustle and bustle of the crowd. See as much detail as possible, and feel an eager anticipation to meet the challenge that awaits you. If you're not used to meditating, visualizing might seem difficult at first. Persist, as you've done with your physical training.

Test Your Prerace Meal

The weeks before a race are a good time to experiment with your ideal prerace meal. Try eating a high-carbohydrate snack, such as a bagel and banana, 60 to 90 minutes before a moderate to long workout to ensure you don't experience nausea. Another good prerace meal is an energy bar containing about 40 to 50 grams of carbohydrate with 8 ounces of water 60 to 90 minutes before the race. If you do experience nausea, your stomach might be sensitive. Try something else, or try timing your prerace meal so that you eat it as long as two hours before you start exercising.

Some sports products are specifically designed to be easily digestible, such as several of the products we covered in chapter 8. You might want to test out some of these as preevent meals during your training:

- A carbohydrate loading and recovery drink
- A balanced nutrition shake with plenty of carbohydrate, moderate protein, and low fat content
- Carbohydrate gels and energy bars

Practice Your Transitions

Now is a good time to practice your swim-to-bike transition, known as T1 in tri-speak, and your bike-to-run transition, known as, you guessed it, T2.

Practice your T1 transitions on a beach. Set up a mock transition area at an open-water swim site and have somebody watch your stuff while you swim. Lay everything you're going to need on a towel, just like you will do at the race transition area (I'll give you a checklist later in this chapter). Don't make this a long workout. Swim a short distance, practice getting out of your wetsuit (if you'll be wearing one), change into your bike gear, and go for a short ride.

Practice your T2 transition on another day. Again, set up a mock transition area, but this time you can set it up on your doorstep. Go for a short bike ride, and then change into your running gear and go for a short run. Although you should have already done some brick workouts, these practices should help you make smooth transitions and get used to the gear and clothing (if any) changes. You should also decide how you want to approach the transitions. Essentially, there are two ways of transitioning: the fast way and the comfortable way.

The Fast Way

The fast way means racing in your swimsuit. The benefit is obvious: a quick transition. The drawbacks are also obvious: saddle soreness and, if it's a cool day, goose bumps. As I've mentioned before, most competitive triathletes competing in sprint- or Olympic-distance triathlons choose to go this route. Riding in a swimsuit is tolerable for most people for these relatively short distances, and if you've wisely purchased a triathlon swimsuit with some padding, that will help as well.

The Comfortable Way

If you have personal reasons for not riding and running in your swimsuit or feel that bike shorts will make a big difference in terms of comfort, then by all means, take your time and slip them on over your swimsuit. (Most triathlons of shorter distances don't have changing areas, and being naked in the transition area is cause for disqualification and possible arrest!) Feel free to stop and don cycling shorts, cycling jersey, and any other clothing that you feel will help you maintain comfort. Of course, all that extra dressing will add to your transition time. But if you're just doing the triathlon to finish, who cares?

Whether you run with or without socks depends on how sensitive your feet are. Again, most triathletes forgo this for shorter distances, but that doesn't mean you have to. An inexpensive and helpful item to make your running shoe transition quick are lace locks or similar quick-locking laces devices. These attach to your shoelaces and make tying your shoes as simple as tightening the laces and pulling down. They are surprisingly solid and dependable, tightening your laces as well as a double knot. Some specialty triathlon running shoes come with something like this built in, but if yours do not, consider it a low-cost, time-saving investment.

Unless you feel an insatiable need to show off your new duds, there's really no need for running shorts. One exception may be if you're wearing bulky cycling shorts, which may chafe your groin area and be a nuisance on the run. If that's the case, go ahead and put on those running shorts over your swimsuit (most short- to medium-triathlon transition areas do not have a changing area, although ducking into a port-a-potty is always an option, albeit a nasally offensive one).

If you plan to change gear during transitions, be sure to practice it before the day of the big race.

Measuring Up

Courtesy of Christian Racoma.

For some people, the motivation to dive into triathlon is that it can be an accurate measuring stick of progress. For Christian Racoma, it was a tool for improving his health and a way for him to ensure that he was making strides forward.

Christian has been an avid weightlifter since his youth, but as he hit his mid-30s, he started to take a more mature perspective on exercise. "I became less concerned about looking good for the sake of looking good and more concerned about my heart health, cholesterol levels, and body fat. But I didn't want to just run farther and faster. I needed a gauge, a measurement."

So Christian signed up for his first triathlon, joining a beginners' triathlon training group, and taking a swimming class at his local gym to help shore up his aquatic skills and overcome his jitters in the water. That helped boost his confidence, since most in the class were nervous about doing their first triathlon as well, especially the swim leg.

Today the 39-year resident of Chicago has seven triathlons under his belt and has embraced a triathlon lifestyle. He also continues to look on multisports as a health report card of sorts.

"With weightlifting, you have an immediate and visible measurement of improvement—big, toned muscles you can see in the mirror. With cardio, I needed a reason to exercise with a bigger goal in mind, or else I knew it would be too easy to skip a workout. Triathlon has forced me to work out more consistently. My measurement of health and fitness isn't how big my biceps are anymore. Now, it's my personal best during a triathlon."

His advice for first-time triathletes who might be nervous about how they'll measure up on race day? "The most important thing to remember on race day is to relax and enjoy the experience. Remember, your goal is just to finish. Once you get through the swim part, you can coast on the bike, if you need to, and walk a portion of the run leg, if you want. You'll have a successful day just by finishing your very first triathlon."

Finalize Travel Arrangements

Will you be traveling to your race? If so, are there any special travel arrangements you need to make, such as confirming hotel reservations? Make arrangements well in advance so that you're not worrying about these details the day before a race.

Don't Make Any Equipment Changes

Now is *not* the time to make any equipment changes, such as a new bike or a different saddle position. If you've been training with no problems with your current equipment and bike position, then there's no reason to change. Changing these factors in the weeks before a race could hurt you or, worse, cause injury. Even swimming goggles can take a few workouts to fit your face properly, so stick with what you've got now unless you absolutely have to change because of breakage, theft, or some other factor that necessitates replacement.

You might be able to get away with purchasing new running shoes two weeks before an event, but one week would be stretching it.

Today's running shoes don't take as long to break in as older models did because of high-tech materials and design. Still, it's best to be on the safe side unless you absolutely need to replace them.

Many triathlons hold expos the day before the event takes place, and often you can get great deals on bicycle stuff and multisport products. Many novice triathletes get carried away and purchase new equipment they intend to use the next day. Don't do it! Sure, go ahead and snag some great steals, but save it for the next event. Always train with new equipment before you race with it.

What to Do Days Before the Race

The few days preceding your first triathlon can be a little nerve-wracking. For the water-challenged, feelings of impending doom might haunt you, and butterflies may occasionally flutter around in your stomach. Even if you've done a few multisport events, any new, challenging, or longer distance race can have a similar effect.

These feelings are completely normal. Find comfort in the pages of your triathlon logbook (you've been keeping one, haven't you?). You've done the homework, and though you might be nervous, you'll do just fine. Talk to training partners and other triathletes who have been through it. Log onto any triathlon chat room on the Internet and seek reassurance. If you've trained properly, you'll have a wonderful experience.

Besides taking care of your mental state, here are a few other reminders and suggestions for the days before a race:

- **Do a safety check on your bike.** The one piece of equipment most likely to break down is your bike, so you'd be smart to do a safety check. Look for any parts that might have loosened through the countless miles of training you've put in. Tighten your stem, aerobars, seatpost, pedals—anything that might be loose. Check your brakes, and look for any cuts or slits in your tires. If you're not mechanically inclined, take your bike to a local shop that you trust, but make sure they can do a quick safety check of your bike while you wait. You don't want to be stuck the night before a race with your bike in the shop.

- **Eat well.** Pay special attention to your diet in the days preceding your race. Stay away from high-fat foods and try not to eat too late. Eat healthy snacks. Focus on eating high-carbohydrate meals. Drink plenty of liquids.

TO LOAD OR NOT TO LOAD

You've probably heard of carbohydrate loading, which is described briefly in chapter 8. The idea behind carbohydrate loading is simple. As we discussed, carbohydrate is the best source of glycogen, a clean-burning fuel ideally suited for high-energy efforts. The problem is that, like a gas tank in a car, our muscles can only hold so much glycogen before they run dry.

When that happens, look out. After about 20 miles in a marathon you might "hit the wall," or more specifically, feel like a Mack truck flattened you. You might lose energy and feel overwhelming fatigue or nausea—any number of different, unpleasant symptoms depending on your body's physiology. Although this physiological phenomenon is somewhat different in bicycling, cyclists often refer to this experience as bonking. It feels just like it sounds, folks. Your tongue might be hanging over your handlebar, and if you haven't gotten enough liquids, the inside of your mouth might feel fur lined.

The purpose of carbohydrate loading is to offset (and possibly avoid) such occurrences in events lasting over two hours. In effect, you are trying to create a bigger gas tank, a greater reserve of glycogen to delay running on fumes. Notice that I said events lasting over two hours. If you're getting ready to complete a sprint-distance triathlon, you don't need to carbo-load. Even for an Olympic-distance race, the benefits of carbo-loading are negligible.

If you're training regularly and eating a diet composed mainly of carbohydrate, just keep doing what you're doing because you're already carbohydrate loading to some degree. (That was easy, huh?) The process of pushing your body harder and harder every day, with proper rest and recovery and in conjunction with a high-carbohydrate diet, increases the capacity of your muscles to hold glycogen reserves. Taking advantage of the carbohydrate window and ingesting carbohydrate immediately after exercise (as discussed in chapter 8) also helps the body to hold more glycogen reserves in the future.

- **Pick up your race packet.** Some races require you or give you the option of picking up your race number, T-shirt, and goodie bag the day before the race. If not, you'll have to sort through that stuff on race morning.

- **Attend prerace meetings.** Many major races hold a prerace meeting the day before the event. Even if attendance is not required, it's a good idea for novice triathletes to attend. These meetings typically cover topics such as water temperature, course descriptions, rules, grounds for disqualification, and other important information.

- **Make sure you know the wheres and whens.** Do you know the directions to the race site? Do you know where to park? What time does your age group wave start? All of this information should be covered in your race packet, if you get it the day before. If not, make sure you contact the race office and get this information a few days before. Don't wait until the night before; more often than not, the race office staff is out setting up the course or too busy to handle your call.

- **Prepare everything the night before.** Give yourself a few hours the night before a race to get all your gear together. Don't wait until after midnight to be scrambling around, putting your stuff together. If you've picked up your race packet, pin your number to a piece of clothing you'll be wearing, and tie in any number cards or place stickers the race folks might have given you to put on your bike or helmet. Many triathletes who race in their swimsuit use a race belt, an elastic belt that you can pin your number to and that quickly snaps around your waist. If you'll be using one, pin your race number to it.

  Set out the clothing you'll be wearing on race morning. This should include your swimsuit, which will go on underneath whatever you'll be wearing as you head out to the race. Pack a gym bag of everything you'll need for the race. Use the checklist on page 155 to make sure you don't forget anything.

Get a Good Night's Sleep

Make sure you request a wake-up call or set your alarm so that you have plenty of time to get ready for the big race day. You don't want to be rushing, which will only add to the nervousness you might already feel on race morning. Do whatever relaxes you before you go to bed: listen to music, soak in the tub, have a hot cup of tea. Try to get to bed early. It might take awhile before the jitters wear off and you fall asleep. If, despite all your efforts, you get to bed late or the jitters keep you up, try not to worry too much about your lack of sleep. Just do your best to get as much sleep and relaxation as you can so that you're mentally alert and ready for the big day with a good attitude.

RACE BAG CHECKLIST

I've found the best way to make sure I've packed everything I need for racing is to break down triathlon gear by category, which I've narrowed down to four:

Swim Gear

Swimsuit (place this with the clothes you'll be wearing race morning)

Goggles

Antifog drops for goggles (optional)

Wetsuit (optional)

Swim cap (the race has probably provided one for you)

Bike Gear

Helmet (make sure you attach any race number stickers that might have been provided)

Bike shoes (optional)

Socks (optional for shorter races)

Cycling shorts (optional for shorter races)

Cycling jersey (optional for shorter races)

Cycling glasses (optional, but recommended)

Water bottles (filled with water or a sports drink)

Spare tubes

Tools

Running Gear

Running shoes

Race number (attached to a race belt or your running shorts, T-shirt, or singlet)

Socks (optional)

Running shorts (optional for shorter races)

Running T-shirt or singlet (optional for shorter races)

Headband, visor, or cap (optional)

Sunglasses (optional)

Race Support Gear

Sport watch

Sports drink, energy bars, or snacks

Jacket (in case of rain or cool weather)

Sport sunscreen

Water-based lubricant (to rub in areas where wetsuit chafing may occur or during running and cycling)

Towel (to set out everything you need during the race and provide a place to sit during your transitions)

The Five Most Common Mistakes to Avoid

We've already covered some of the mistakes you'll want to avoid, such as poor nutrition before the race or training too hard right before the event. Here are a few other typical prerace bloopers you'll want to avoid . . .

- **Overreacting to new race course information.** It's important to be familiar with the race course on race day, but don't squeeze in some last-minute training based on new information you learn about the race the day before the event. For example, perhaps you discover that the bike course is hillier than you thought—now is not the time to get in some last-minute hill training. You'll risk injury or burnout, plus it won't do you much good, anyway.

- **Losing sleep.** Chances are you'll be a little anxious the days before your first triathlon. While it's not a big deal to get less sleep the night before, long-term sleep deprivation over three or more days can cause you to lose your edge and diminish your enjoyment on race day. Make a special effort to catch up on your sleep the week before an event. This will also help your body recover from training.

- **Becoming *too* preoccupied with details.** Triathlon racing, like life, is a balancing act. We've talked about the importance of covering all those details, but there is such a thing as obsessing over insignificant particulars. Examples include fussing over the lack of detail on the swim course map, fretting over which flavor Gatorade to drink, and checking the race Web site every 15 minutes.

- **Not accounting for race-day conditions.** Keep an eye on the weather forecast in the days before the race. If there's even a slight chance of rain, pack a poncho for prerace transition area setup and comfort. If conditions will be hot and humid, pack extra fluids and your best moisture-wicking racing apparel. Of course, don't forget your sunblock and sunglasses.

- **Not preparing for a flat.** We've talked about the importance of having the essential flat repair equipment on your bicycle—tube, frame air pump, tire levers. Yet, you'll almost always see a novice triathlete walking his or her bicycle back to the transition area or waiting for a rescue wagon during a big race. Don't let that be you. You should have done it long ago, but if you haven't, visit your bike shop for the gear and a flat-tire changing lesson the week before the race.

Mental Prep:
Accessing Goals and Expectations

You've no doubt thought about, maybe even obsessed over, your potential race time or age group placing. Again, if this is your first triathlon, your race time is unimportant.

Poor race performance excuse #51: Abducted by space aliens.

As a society, we place too much emphasis on performance and not enough on the experience. If you're a first-timer, just enjoy yourself and finish the race safely and in good spirits.

To help put yourself in a relaxed and positive frame of mind, here are some simple thought-provoking questions to consider in the days before a race.

> How important is your race time compared to the benefits you've gained from the experience of training for your first triathlon in the last few months to a year?

> Why did you first decide do a triathlon? What was the personal, deep motivation?

> Are you a type-A person? Do you tend to push yourself too hard or have extraordinary expectations for yourself? If so, could your first triathlon be a stage for starting to teach yourself to enjoy the process and not focus so much on outcomes?

> Ultimately, what do you want to get out of triathlon?

To get the most out of these questions, write your answers in your workout diary or personal journal. Doing so will reinforce a positive perspective when it comes to your expectation about your first race and beyond.

Once you've completed your first triathlon, use a journal to record your thoughts about how you did in each race, comparing your experience from one event to the next. As you become more experienced, the insights you'll garner from journaling will prove invaluable.

chapter 11

Nailing the Big Day

It's all right to have butterflies in your stomach.
Just get them to fly in formation.

—Dr. Rob Gilbert

There's something truly special about race-day morning. It's a mixture of nervousness, excitement, energy, and, if it's your first triathlon, a pervading apprehension about delving into something mysterious and unknown. You'll no doubt feel a sense of pride, and hopefully you'll have some loved ones tagging along to show their support and appreciation. Here you are . . . a triathlete. Ready to swim, ride, and run alongside a tribe of common people with an uncommon commitment to fitness and life. Yes, you will feel many things on race day. Enjoy it. You'll likely have many more triathlons in your future . . . but you will have only one first.

What to Do on Race Morning

Unless you're the bravest man or woman in the world, you'll probably be pretty nervous. Just relax and focus on getting everything in your car that you need for the race. If time permits, try to do something relaxing—listen to music, or ask your spouse nicely ("Please, honey") to massage your shoulders and scalp.

- **Time your prerace meal.** Almost all of us have had some stomach distress, be it nausea, side stitches, or diarrhea, during exercise. Although during a race these conditions can often be attributed to nervousness, at times they are caused by eating a prerace meal too close to the start. As indicated in chapter 8, it's important to eat your prerace meal well before the race—at least an hour before the start or, for sensitive stomachs or bigger meals, as long as two hours before the start.

- **Plan to race with tried and tested gear, nutrition, and apparel.** We've talked about how important it is not to try out new gear or nutrition on race day; the same goes for your race outfit. You might have picked out a fancy new tri-suit at a prerace expo, but, if you haven't trained in it, you might find it uncomfortable, or worse, chafing. Make sure that you've tested your apparel in training and that it's comfortable.

- **Get to the transition area one hour before the start.** First-timers might even want to get there 90 minutes or two hours before the start, especially if it's a city event with huge participation numbers. Getting there early gives you plenty of time to park and walk to the transition area (in big events, you might park as much as a mile from the race site). Triathlons, especially the large urban events, can be a bear to get to and find parking at on race morning. If your drive from your home or hotel is a long distance, you might run into traffic. And lines at port-a-potties can be brutal. Plan for these contingencies and give yourself a nice time cushion for something to go wrong, or simply to do a relaxed warm-up or mental visualization session.

- **Park your bike and get your body marked.** When you walk your bike and carry your gym bag to the transition area, you'll most likely be greeted by security personnel who will ask to see your race number. Park your bike on the bike racks provided; hang your bicycle handlebars over the railing. In many races, bike rack positions are preassigned according to your race number, so look for your number and park your bike there. Before you start unpacking your gym bag, seek out body markers, race volunteers who will write your race number on your arms and legs. These numbers help identify you when you're coming out of the swim and onto the bike.

- **Set up your personal transition station.** Lay out your towel next to your bike. Don't be a hog about space—just use enough room to set out your gear. Place your cycling and running gear in logical progression, with the cycling stuff on the half of the towel closest to you. Make sure everything is easily accessible. The photo on page 161 is a good example of an organized transition area.

- **Relax.** It's normal to compare yourself to others, especially when you're the new kid on the block and about to toe the line with experienced triathletes. As

A well-organized transition area allows you to stay focused on your performance, not your gear, when time is crucial during the race.

a newcomer, you might not have the sleekest bicycle or the newest apparel or gear, but who cares? You'll quickly notice on race day that everybody is pretty much focused on the task at hand, not on how anybody looks. (Besides, does anybody really look good wearing a swimsuit and helmet on a bicycle?)

- **Get ready to swim.** If you're wearing a wetsuit, slip it on. Dab some water-based lubricant in areas that might chafe, such as armpits and groin. No need to zip up the top half if the race won't start for awhile and it's a hot day. Check your goggle straps and have your swim cap ready.

- **Check out the lay of the land.** Once you've got your gear organized and you're ready to swim, take a walk around the transition area.

    1. Notice where your bike is racked. Are there any distinguishable markers or landmarks that will help you find your bike quickly after the swim? Some triathletes bring balloons or colorful flags to help with this issue, but all you really need is some permanent landmark near your bike. Another option is to count the number of bike rack rows to your bike from the swim-to-bike transition area entrance.

    2. Find out where you'll be exiting the transition area on your bike and where you'll be exiting on the run. Make a mental note of these

directions. Volunteers are sometimes positioned in the transition area to point the way for groggy, disoriented, or tired triathletes, but don't depend on help.

3. Walk to the beach to get a feel for the swim course from shore. You should have some knowledge of the shape of the swim course from the race information provided to you, but it helps to have a look for yourself. Will the swim buoys always be on your right or left? How many turns will you make? If it's a hazy day and you can't tell from the shore, ask any nearby race official.

Overcoming Prerace Jitters

On the morning of your first triathlon it's natural to be nervous, and if you don't have a case of the prerace jitters, you might want to check your pulse. Stay focused on what you need to do in the critical hours and minutes to prepare for the start of the race.

Having a case of the jitters can cause you to forget a piece of gear, such as your bicycle helmet, which will get you disqualified and ruin your inaugural triathlon party. So accept that you'll likely be nervous and jumpy, but make all the preparations and use checklists to ensure it doesn't get in the way of your final preparation. Enlist the help of a significant other to watch your back and make sure you don't forget anything you need for the race.

Here are a few tips that, time permitting, might help steady your nerves on race morning:

- Take a solitary stroll away from the transition area and think of all the training you've done to get to this point.
- Bring some headphones and listen to a few of your favorite songs to soothe you.
- Socialize with other triathletes you know who are also racing for the first time—sharing your nervousness will help calm you.
- Plan on a prerace bathroom break. Although race directors do their best to accommodate participants, port-a-potty lines can be pretty long, so get there early.
- As you wait for your wave's turn on the beach, close your eyes for a few moments and visualize a smooth, uneventful, and fun swim experience.

What to Do (and Not Do) During a Race

As with anything in life, a myriad of things can go wrong during a race: a kick in the head during the swim, a flat tire during the bike ride, a blister on your foot during the run. Solid preparation beforehand will help minimize surprises. Another key to having a good race is intelligently handling the variables you can control.

Keep Your Head During the Swim

Even if you do seed yourself properly, body contact can still occur during the swim. It might be as mildly unsettling as grazing another swimmer's arm with yours or as startling as a kick in the face. Keep your wits about you and be aware of other swimmers in your immediate area. If you do have the misfortune of playing open-water swimming's version of bumper cars, keep calm and make adjustments. If you have to, stop and tread water, letting other swimmers too close to you go by (but be careful that nobody swims into you from behind). If you are a particularly slow swimmer (like me), be prepared for the fast fish in the waves behind you to come zooming by like speedboats. Again, be aware of them, keep calm, and let them pass without incident.

Prepare for Smooth Transitions

Triathlon is a paradox. You need to be in the present moment to race your best, but you also need to mentally and physically prepare for what comes next. (Is that philosophical, or what?) Transitions give you that window of opportunity to jump to the next activity, but even transitions require a little forethought.

T1 Tips

Triathletes often feel disoriented and uncoordinated at the swim-to-bike transition. That's especially true if you're new to open water or just had a rough swim. These tips can help you make a smooth T1:

- In the few yards before you come to shore, mentally envision a smooth transition.
- Be prepared for possible dizziness when you stand up.
- Ease your pace in the last few yards so that you don't jump out of the water breathless.
- When you're in shallow water close to the beach, gradually adjust to your "sea legs" by propping yourself on your knees, then slowly feeling the land under your feet.
- Unzip your wetsuit as you walk or run to your bike.
- Look for your landmark or count the number of rows to your bike.
- Drink some fluids.
- Don't forget to strap on your helmet before you get on your bike or else you'll be disqualified.
- Carefully walk or ride your bike out of the transition area, depending on what the race policy is (if you aren't sure, play it safe and walk your bike out).

T2 Tips

By far, the T2 transition is the hardest for the first-timer. Although brick workouts should have helped you get accustomed to that tight feeling of coming off the bike and starting to run, nothing quite prepares you for the real thing. Some people have no trouble with T2, but others deal with cramping and nonexistent runner's legs. These tips can help you make a smooth T2:

- Drink plenty—cramping during T2 could signal dehydration.
- A mile or so before the end of the ride, back off and pedal in an easier gear.
- Concentrate on smooth pedal strokes and stretching out your leg muscles.
- Mentally prepare to make the transition to running.
- Be slow and cautious when entering the transition area—most bicycle accidents occur here.
- If your legs are very tight, stretch them.
- Begin running slowly with short strides, easing into it and increasing your pace as your leg muscles allow.

TRANSITION SETUP TIPS

Here are some tips to make your T1 and T2 go more smoothly.

- Have a water bottle handy for a quick sip after the swim.
- If you're going to wear cycling shoes, undo the straps or laces so that you won't have to fumble around with them.
- Fill all your water bottles on the bike.
- Put your bike in an easy gear for a quick start.
- Place your cycling glasses inside your helmet so that you don't forget to put them on.
- If you've opted for socks on the bike or run, put them in your shoes.
- Loosen your running shoelaces for quick entry.
- Place the race belt (or whatever article of clothing you've attached your race number to) next to your sunglasses, cap, or anything else you'll be wearing on the run.
- Take a quick prerace dip. Most races allow a warm-up, as long as you get out of the way when the race begins. A prerace dip helps offset some of the initial shock of the water (especially if temps are a bit chilly) and is especially helpful for those wearing wetsuits. A thin layer of water will seep into the wetsuit (which is normal) and create a warming barrier for you, if given enough time to be heated by your body. However, don't wear yourself out with a long swim. You might see other triathletes swimming, or possibly even cycling or running, but best to save your energy for the race.
- Seed yourself properly in your swim wave. Very few races have mass starts these days, so you'll most likely be swimming with people in your age group. If you are a novice swimmer, have any reservations about open-water swimming, or are competing in your first triathlon, position yourself at the back of the pack or off to the side. This way, you'll avoid unnecessary body contact.

Stick to the Plan (and the Pace)

It's easy to get so caught up in the hoopla of a race: the huge crowd, the balloons and banners, the noise and music. When the gun (or cannon or horn) goes off, you're so shot up with adrenaline that it's hard to hold yourself back. And if the kids or your significant other is watching, well, you're raring to show 'em just how fast daddy or mommy or sweetheart can tear up the triathlon course. Don't do it! You might look impressive during those first few minutes of the swim or from the transition to the bike or run, but you'll soon start to feel the effects before you reach the first buoy or mile marker.

One of the most difficult things for triathletes to learn is pacing. Each of us has an internal clock, and even during the excitement of a race, we can learn to run by that clock and knock off the miles with consistent and strong splits. The key is to minimize any external influences that can affect your internal clock and sense of pace. Stick to your plan. If you're just racing to finish, don't send your body into oxygen deprivation by sprinting. If performance is on your mind, stay true to the pace that will get you there in the time you want, but also be flexible in case your arms or legs just don't have it.

Drink Plenty of Fluids

In chapters 6 and 8 we discussed heat illnesses and how to avoid them, but it's worth noting that it's necessary to drink fluids during a race as well. Even veteran triathletes can get carried away in the heat of the moment and neglect to down enough fluids (until they end up befriending an IV bottle in the medical tent). The biggest key to avoiding dehydration and heat illness is to stay properly hydrated. Drink fluids immediately after the swim and drink eight ounces of water or a sports drink every 15 minutes while you ride. During the run, take advantage of every water station.

Do you need to eat during a race? For sprint-distance races, probably not. For Olympic-distance races or longer, eating a carbohydrate gel or solid snack is a good idea (of course, these foods should have already been tested for digestibility during training).

Have Fun

The best advice is to have fun out there. Don't take it too seriously and kill yourself. Be courteous and kind to your race colleagues, volunteers, police officers, and spectators. If you intend to make triathlon a healthy and fun lifestyle choice instead of a one-shot, grueling event, keep a big smile on your face as you race. It'll be even bigger when you finish.

What to Do After the Race for Fast Recovery

The triathlon finish line is a place where dreams are fulfilled. But it's also a place where you have to be pragmatic about recovering from your hard effort. The things

you do and don't do in the minutes and hours after a triathlon will lead to a quick and painless recovery or will cause you to stumble around and sneeze in the next few months. Paying attention to recovery strategies after your finish can help you get back on your feet quickly. Most important, these recovery tips can help you avoid injury and sickness.

Tip 1: Keep Moving

When you cross the finish line, you might want to plonk down on the first spot you find, but that will hurt your chances for a fast recovery. Continue walking on your feet for 5 to 15 minutes. This will bring your heart rate down gradually, since you've been racing for an extended time. Walking will also help disperse some of the lactic acid in your muscles. You might have to stop to have a finish chute volunteer tear off the bottom stub of your race number, but keep moving as soon as that's done.

If there is a logjam of people in the finishing chutes and you're forced to come to a complete stop, walk in place without lifting your knees up too high. You can also try some light stretching, but be careful and keep your movement slow and your range of motion limited. Overstretching in your current taxed state can activate reflexes in exhausted muscles that could cause cramping or injury, so take it slow and easy. Focus your stretching on large muscle groups, such as hamstrings and quadriceps, holding until you feel a slight strain for 15 to 30 seconds. If you feel your muscles tensing, immediately stop stretching and continue to walk.

Living Her Dream and Helping Others

Courtesy of OU Medical Center, Oklahoma City.

By any objective measurement, Dr. Amanda Stevens is successful in every part of her life. And, as with many gifted people, her talents are broad based. From her natural athleticism to the accomplishments she's made during her medical career, Amanda brings passion and energy to everything she does, including a very active community service agenda.

She grew up in a family of swimmers— Amanda and her three siblings all swam on the national level in high school and went on to successful swimming careers in college. During medical school, she was encouraged by her peers to do a triathlon, but she was an unwilling convert. "I was adamant that I don't bike or run. 'I am a swimmer,' I would tell my friend, but, after a lot of persuasion, I entered my first triathlon."

Her lack of biking and running training notwithstanding, Amanda had extraordinary success in her first few triathlons in 2001, so much that she qualified for the USAT national championships. She ended up winning her age group at nationals and was top 10 overall. For the next few years, Amanda spent blocks of time finishing medical school and training and having great success in triathlon, including racing at the 2002 world championships and winning her age group. She graduated from medical school in 2006 and also continues to compete as a pro. She just missed qualifying for the 2008 Olympics.

But what's most impressive about Amanda is her dedication to community service. Amanda is a speaker for Making It Count, a high school program sponsored by many Fortune 500 companies that reaches over 2 million students annually. Her goal is to teach kids and teens healthy lifestyle habits. And one of the primary mantras she instills in kids is pretty simple: "Set goals. And start each goal with the two most powerful words of the English language when used together: *I will*."

Amanda continues to compete professionally in triathlon; she raced in her first 70.3 race in 2008, placing second and qualifying for the world championships.

Her advice for first-time triathletes during race day: "Have fun and enjoy what you are doing. All the work and preparation you put into training means you get to go enjoy the race. Stay in the moment and give it your best so you will be able to walk away from any race satisfied with your efforts and accomplishments."

Tip 2: Drink Up!

Even if you hit all the aid stations during the race, you should continue to hydrate with a sports drink after you finish. Complete restoration of the fluids and electrolytes (potassium and sodium) lost after a hard endurance effort is an important component of recovery. This is doubly true in hot or humid conditions.

According to the Gatorade Sports Science Institute, a good rule is to drink 16 ounces (about half a liter) of fluid per pound (half a kilogram) of body weight lost. But since you'd be hard pressed to find a bathroom scale at the start and finish line, just drink a reasonable amount of fluids after the race: for example, 16 to 24 ounces (.5 to .7 L) of sports drink in the first 15 minutes and 8 to 16 ounces (.25 to .5 L) thereafter.

Tip 3: Take Advantage of the Carbohydrate Window

As you recall from chapter 8, researchers view the carbohydrate window as a critical time to ingest carbohydrate. When you do so during those first two hours after a race, it helps replace muscle glycogen twice as fast as normal. Even a small snack like a banana or energy bar will help your recovery. If none of these high-carbohydrate foods appeals to you, then, at the minimum, eat whatever you crave. After all, you deserve it, and it might be your body telling you what it's lacking.

In addition, a moderate amount of protein can aid in recovery. Most energy bars contain some protein, so having one on hand at the finish line is a good idea. A sports drink and a high-carbohydrate, moderate-protein energy bar are the perfect finish-line foods for recovery. Another alternative is a carbohydrate-and-protein shake.

Tip 4: Eat Healthy and Take Supplements

Your immune system is weak after a triathlon, especially a long-distance event, so it's important to eat healthy. Later that evening and throughout the week, have an all-natural dinner consisting of complex carbohydrate, like vegetables and whole grains, much like you should have enjoyed in the few days before the event. The goal is to continue to completely replenish lost muscle glycogen, which can take as long as a week. Dishes should be composed of 60 to 70 percent carbohydrate with moderate amounts of protein and fat.

It wouldn't hurt to take some immunity-boosting supplements, such as vitamin C, garlic, vitamin E, or an antioxidant blend. It's common for endurance athletes to catch a cold within days after an event. Also, if it's a cool day, have some warm clothes nearby to protect yourself from the chills.

Postrace Thoughts: How to Evaluate Your Performance

You'll likely have a lot of feelings and emotions about how you performed in your triathlon. How you come away from a competition—emotionally—has dramatic effects on your subsequent performances and commitment (or lack thereof) to the sport on a long-term basis. In chapter 12 we'll talk about ways to ensure that triathlon becomes not just something you do, but also a lifestyle. For now, consider how you should evaluate your race-day performance. One of the best ways to do this is by separating what really happened out there from your emotions.

- **Separate myth from fact.** Take a sheet of paper and draw a line down the middle. On the left side, write a factual account of the event. These should include things such as splits, weather conditions, mechanical problems, race-course conditions, heart rate, and any other factors that you can recall.

- **How did you feel?** On the right side, write down your reactions to the facts. How did you feel during each portion of the event? Describe your moods, thoughts, and self-criticisms that were going through your head.

- **Compare.** Look at the facts on the left side and your judgments and emotions on the right side. Ask yourself these questions: Did I expect to do better? Were those realistic expectations? Though I might not have reached my highest expectations, did I achieve any other objectives?

- **Focus on the positive.** Write a race report that includes any positive facts that surfaced. Leave out the emotional judgments. Compare what you wrote with your feelings during the race or any negative feelings you might have now about the event.

This kind of postrace analysis can help you not only with your first race but with every race after that. It can aid you in evaluating your performance honestly and in your process of self-discovery and introspection.

chapter 12

Tri, Tri Again

Learn to act as though the life you visualize is already here.

—Dr. Wayne Dyer

Bongarts/SportsChrome

Like any sport, triathlon has several unspoken and undocumented rules. These codes of ethics are not spelled out in the USA Triathlon handbook, but they are just as applicable to triathletes.

Among the running and triathlon community, for example, there's the race T-shirt rule: Never wear a race T-shirt unless you've finished that race. Dropped out? Got sick? Lightning hit you on the way to the finish line? Then give the shirt to your neighbor. Use it to clean your bike chain. Burn it. Just don't wear the shirt if you haven't done the race.

Among my circle of multisport friends, we have the "license to call yourself a triathlete" rule. This rule stipulates that you must complete at least one triathlon a year to continue to refer to yourself as a triathlete. No matter how much running, cycling, or swimming you've done during training, you've got to prove your mettle on a race course at least once every 365 days. The one exception to this rule is the "lifetime Ironman license" amendment. Should you finish an Ironman-distance event, you are awarded a lifetime license to call yourself a triathlete, even if you never do another race.

Yet none of my friends who have completed an Ironman race have stopped competing or taken a hiatus from training (including me). Although I planned to take a yearlong respite from multisport training after my Ironman finish, I just couldn't do it. The running shoes beckoned. Roads ripe for cycling called for more adventures. The sweet sensation of cool open waters lured me.

During a particularly satisfying run on a pristine trail recently, I realized why I couldn't take time away from multisport training. *This is who I am.* At some point in my 15 years of swimming, biking, and running, triathlon had become an integral part of me. I could no sooner walk away from it for a year than I could stop writing.

Being a Triathlon Lifer

Chances are, you've chosen to participate in multisport events because they challenge you in a way no other activity can. Unlike the common one-time marathoners, triathletes usually come back for more, and more, and more.

Besides the fun and variety that triathlon training and racing provide, I believe triathletes are lifers because of the inevitable positive effects swimming, biking, and running have on their lives. Although triathlon is not the definitive answer to everyone's problems, here are some of the changes and influences you might find happening in your life as a result of triathlon:

- **Shedding bad habits.** Hey, we all have them—those things we do to ourselves that aren't really good for us but have turned into habits from years of reinforcement. Embracing multisports can be the impetus for unloading some of that annoying baggage. It could be as dramatic as quitting smoking or something more subtle like stopping overeating, partying all night, or just being too sedentary. You might find yourself not watching as much television and getting outdoors more.

- **Better eating habits.** Something about being fit naturally translates into taking a good look at the foods you eat. Meals are no longer just an opportunity to feed your face; they are a chance to refuel from a hard day's workout. Naturally, you want the best fuel you can get so that tomorrow's workout goes well. If excessive body weight is an issue for you, you'll find that triathlon is a great way to burn calories.

- **Healthier sleeping patterns.** You might find that you sleep better at night, with less interruption of sleep (if you don't work out just before you go to bed and don't overtrain). A good day's training might also require that you get a little more sleep, which can only help you.

- **More friends.** Triathlon is a great social sport. No doubt, you'll meet people with similar goals and philosophies and start some lifelong friendships. If you take my advice and go to swim camp and do group rides and runs, you'll have plenty of opportunities to meet like-minded people.

Triathlon is a lifestyle sport with many health benefits that will keep you feeling great your entire life.

- **Less sickness, more energy.** Studies have shown that regular, moderate exercise (not excessive, as in overtraining) can help boost your immune system. You might also feel more energetic during the day, and working out can help recharge you when your batteries are low.

- **Greater self-discipline.** Training regularly and consistently requires you to keep the promises you make to yourself (via your training schedule). This constant reinforcement instills confidence that you can do what you need to do, regardless of how you are feeling. Focusing on a goal and doing the work that it takes to make that goal a reality will do wonders for your self-esteem and self-discipline.

Using Your First Triathlon as a Stepping-Stone

After you've crossed the finish line of your first triathlon and your elation subsides, you might ask yourself, *What now?* It's natural to feel hesitant about what this all means and what to do next. To help cure those postfinish-line blues and move on to the next step, the following sections suggest ways to help turn the end of your first triathlon into a new beginning.

Get Involved in the Sport

There are countless ways to participate in the sport:

- **Subscribe to a triathlon magazine.** Whether you choose *Inside Triathlon*, *Triathlete*, or one of the myriad regional multisport magazines popping up all over the country, subscribing to these periodicals helps you keep abreast of events and trends happening in the sport. You'll also find training columns, equipment reviews, and, if keeping up with pros and top amateurs interests you, race reports. More important, you'll find a calendar section and race ads so you can find out about upcoming races in your area.

- **Join USA Triathlon.** Most triathlons are sanctioned by USA Triathlon, which means you must be a member to participate or purchase a one-day membership for a small fee. If you plan on doing several USA Triathlon–sanctioned races in a year, it's worth joining because you'll end up paying more in one-day memberships than the annual fee. You'll also receive a USA Triathlon publication as well as access to their travel desk and a few other benefits.

- **Join local triathlon clubs.** If you live in or near a major metropolitan area, chances are there's a triathlon club near you. Ask other triathletes or inquire about clubs at local races. Clubs are a great way to socialize and meet training partners.

- **Get online.** There are several triathlon and multisport sites on the Internet, including bulletin boards and chat rooms where you can post questions or opinions to other triathletes around the world.

- **Join the political arena.** Many significant issues (such as those surrounding drafting and officiating) face triathlon, and organizations such as USA Triathlon give triathletes a voice in the future of the sport. It is important that the sport's governing bodies be represented by grassroots triathletes willing to give their time and energy.

- **Volunteer.** Don't wait until you're injured to consider volunteering for a race. Whether you get aid station duty, transition area security, or finish-line cleanup, the important thing is that you give back to the sport all the enjoyment and fun you get out of it. Who knows, maybe someday you'd like to put on your own triathlon and join the ranks of race directors.

- **Be a coach or mentor.** Whether it's through a club or a youth triathlon training camp, the sport always needs good coaches and mentors. Veteran triathlete Bernard Lyles has created and continues to coordinate a triathlon training program for inner-city kids. Through his devotion, and with the help of a team of triathlete volunteers and financial contributions, Lyles helps change the lives of kids growing up in a tough environment. Talk to local triathlon clubs for information on similar coaching or mentoring programs. If there isn't one, you could always start your own!

Set Your Sights on Another Goal

The fun doesn't have to end with your first sprint- or Olympic-distance race. There are plenty of multisport goals you can set your sights on:

- **Go faster.** When you finish your first triathlon it'll be a personal best no matter what your time is. But perhaps you have this little voice inside you that says you can finish the swim faster, hammer the bike harder, and dash through the run without stopping now that you've got the first-time jitters out of your system. Go for it. Try some speedwork, maybe even some interval training. Keep in mind that you'll need to graduate to the next course of triathlon training knowledge to do it safely.

  By reading multisport magazines and books that cover more advanced endurance and triathlon training techniques, you can further your knowledge and broaden your workout arsenal. As you'll no doubt find, you'll be advised to consider integrating strength training into your schedule. And investing in a faster, lighter, more aerodynamic triathlon bicycle might also be on the horizon.

- **Go farther.** Almost 20 years ago, triathlon journalist Mike Plant pegged the Hawaiian Ironman Triathlon as the holy grail for triathletes. The nickname has stuck. To this day, triathletes look upon the shores of Kona as the ultimate proving grounds for their mettle.

You may not now, or ever, have the desire to finish an Ironman-distance race, but perhaps someday the half Ironman might beckon you.

- **Swim, bike, or run.** You might find that you have a talent in one particular sport and prefer to see how well you can do with it. Seven-time Tour de France champion Lance Armstrong was the sprint-distance Triathlon World Champion before he became involved in world-class cycling. Perhaps the prospect of completing a bicycle century ride (100 miles) or running a marathon excites you.

A Glimpse at the Ironman

As a newcomer to the sport, you are probably focused on sprint or Olympic distances, and the Ironman distance might not be on your horizon at all or, at the very least, it's probably a few years away. But it's likely that you have some curiosity about what it takes to do an Ironman-distance event and what it's like to finish such a grueling race. My first Ironman was the Great Floridian race in Clermont, Florida. I have a few training facts and thoughts to share about my experience.

My Ironman Training Snapshot

Before I got on the plane to Florida, I printed out my training totals from the workout log on my computer: 150,000 yards of swimming, 3,500 miles of cycling, and 700 miles of running. In all, I had put in close to 400 hours of training (sounds impressive, but it's actually on the light side for Ironman training). Here are some other facts:

- I gave myself a year to train (with 10 years of multisport experience and a dozen half-Ironman distance finishes to my credit).
- My goal was solely to finish, so my running and cycling training consisted almost entirely of long, slow workouts (base training) designed to simply cover long distances.
- I swam a long swim of an hour or more every other week and concentrated on drills and technique during the remainder of my five weekly pool workouts.
- I put in roughly a dozen 100-mile-plus rides, many of which were organized century rides put on by bike clubs.
- My long runs were between 14 and 21 miles, which I would do once a week.
- My biggest challenge was finding the right saddle (it took me three purchases). After about 50 miles, this makes a big difference!

Beating the Streets

Courtesy of Bernard Lyles.

Bernard Lyles doesn't mess around—the chiseled features of his face, the fierceness in his eyes, and the boom in his voice convey that message. Though he sports a pair of running shorts and a white singlet, the impression is that he might be just as comfortable in a marine uniform.

Lyles isn't a marine commander, but he is in command of an army of almost 100 kids from inner-city Chicago. Lyles is head of the first organized triathlon training program for African American boys and girls. And though they might look like just a bunch of kids running around the training grounds, Lyles is shaping them up and disciplining them for battle, for the determination they'll need in order to deal with the realities of the streets.

Bernard Lyles did his first triathlon in 1983 and has since been instrumental in bringing the sport into the lives of minority adults and youngsters alike. With the aid, support, and motivation of Tri-Masters national founder Alvin Hartley, Lyles founded a Chicago chapter for minority triathletes in 1992. Since then the program has trained over 1,200 youth athletes in the fundamentals of competing in the sport of triathlon. Program participants have competed locally, nationally, and internationally in numerous triathlon and running events.

"If you can channel kids' energy into something positive and away from that nonsense, you can do anything. That's what these kids are learning. With exercise, your mind clears, you think positive thoughts, and all that nonsense goes away."

That "nonsense" refers to gangs firmly entrenched in the community that surrounds this triathlon haven. Lyles knows he can't reach all the kids, and he admits to losing a few to gangs.

"The main thing is to get them off the streets and to learn something. On the streets around here, gangs teach kids to be thugs, drug dealers, or killers. I train these kids to do triathlons because I want them to be something gangs can never teach them. I want them to be athletes."

The Ironman Experience

Everyone experiences an Ironman differently. The one universal experience is a sense of pride and joy in the accomplishment. Having trained just to finish, I approached it in a more relaxed way than more competitive triathletes did. This no-pressure approach helped me to embrace the struggle, as I took the time to thank race volunteers at the aid stations and spectators along the course.

Time has passed since my first Ironman finish. As with most key life experiences, it's easy to dismiss or forget their importance. Yet I count not just crossing the finish line, but the yearlong training and the 15-plus hours it took me to complete the event, as one of the most enjoyable and rewarding times of my life.

Ending Thoughts: It's About Time

Time is a curious thing. As you begin to participate in the sport of triathlon, time can take on a greater significance. You'll no doubt measure the time it takes to swim, T1, bike, T2, and run with apprehension, sometimes with disappointment, and, hopefully, most times with joy.

I read something once about time that fascinated me. The ancient Greeks distinguished time as chronos time or kairos time. Chronos time is clock time, the usual linear way we have of looking at time. As busy human beings living in a harried, hurried society, we continually focus on chronos time. We carry phones that organize our lives into neat little chunks of time and sync with a wireless network. We set our 2,000-function, 100-split memory sport watches to beep at every stride and to catch every mile marker. We can now even latch a GPS tracker onto our shoes or bike handlebars so we know exactly how far and how fast we go.

Kairos time is what some have called soul time. It is usually a time of intensity, of pattern interruption, or of a change in direction. We often don't realize kairos time when it's happening because we're too busy *experiencing* the life-changing belief or revelation. Others characterize kairos time as a shift in perception, a paradigm shift, as author Stephen Covey puts it in *The Seven Habits of Highly Effective People*. Put simply, kairos time is those glorious moments in which you have a deeper understanding of the mystery of life and a fleeting peek into your own soul.

When I look back on my experiences as a triathlete, I realize that I've been fortunate to have had many moments of kairos time—each time I crossed a triathlon finish line. Usually, everything moves in slow motion. I can feel my heartbeat as though it were a tribal drum. Mostly, I experience a pervading sense of wonder at what I can accomplish with a little perseverance.

Those moments are hard to duplicate. Time, like life, is funny that way. But triathlon is one of the few activities we can indulge in where the likelihood of kairos time is much greater, and the possibility of peeking into our own souls for a few quick, sacred moments is there with every splash, mash, and dash. As you embark upon your new multisport adventure, more than wishing you smooth transitions or fast times, I wish you many, many moments of kairos time.

Appendix: Blank Training Grids

The following blank training grids have been provided for your convenience—please feel free to photocopy them for personal use.

My Base Training Schedule

	Swimming	Cycling	Running
Mon			
Tue			
Wed			
Thu			
Fri			
Sat			
Sun			

Tip: Circle or highlight your key workouts.

From J. Mora, 2009, *Triathlon 101*, 2nd ed. (Champaign, IL: Human Kinetics).

My Speed and Technique Training Schedule

	Swimming	Cycling	Running
Mon			
Tue			
Wed			
Thu			
Fri			
Sat			
Sun			

Tip: Don't forget to allow yourself one rest day every week.

From J. Mora, 2009, *Triathlon 101*, 2nd ed. (Champaign, IL: Human Kinetics).

My Race Simulation Training Schedule

	Swimming	Cycling	Running
Mon			
Tue			
Wed			
Thu			
Fri			
Sat			
Sun			

Tip: Practice your navigational skills in open water.

From J. Mora, 2009, *Triathlon 101*, 2nd ed. (Champaign, IL: Human Kinetics).

My Tapering Schedule

	Swimming	Cycling	Running
Mon			
Tue			
Wed			
Thu			
Fri			
Sat			
Sun			

Tip: Remember, don't do any hard or long workouts in the days before a race.

From J. Mora, 2009, *Triathlon 101*, 2nd ed. (Champaign, IL: Human Kinetics).

Bibliography

Connor, W.E. 1978. The plasma lipids, lipoproteins, and diet of the Tarahumaras Indians of Mexico. *American Journal of Clinical Nutrition,* 31:1131-1142.

Covey, S.R. (1989). *The seven habits of highly effective people.* New York: Simon & Schuster.

Coyle, E. 1988. Carbohydrates and athletic performance. *Sports Science Exchange,* 1(7):1-5.

Douillard, J. (1994). *Body, mind and sport.* New York: Harmony.

Ely, M.R., Cheuvront, S.N., Roberts, W.O., Montain, S.J. (2007). Impact of weather on marathon-running performance. *Medicine & Science in Sports & Exercise,* 39(3):487-493.

Galloway, J. (1984). *Galloway's book on running.* Bolinas, CA: Shelter.

Edwards, S. (1992). *Triathlons for fun.* Santa Monica, CA: Triathlete Magazine.

Fixx, J. (1977). *The complete book of running.* New York: Random House.

Hubbard, R.W., Sandick, B.L., Mathew, W.T., Francesconi, R.P., Sampson, J.B., Dorkot, M.J., Maller, O., and Engell, D.B. 1984. Voluntary dehydration and alliesthesia for water. *Journal of Applied Physiology,* 86(1):78-84.

Ivy, J.L., Katz, A.L., Cutler, C.L., Sherman, W.M., and Coyle, E.F. 1988. Muscle glycogen synthesis after exercise: effect of time of carbohydrate ingestion. *Journal of Applied Physiology,* 64:1480.

Laughlin, T. *The guide to fishlike swimming.* New Paltz, NY, 1997.

Mangi, R., Jokl, P., and Dayton, O.W. (1979). *The runner's complete medical guide.* New York: Summit Books.

Mann, M. (1992). Static active stretching training for a healthy back. *The Spine Surgeon,* 12:18.

Mora, J.M. (1991, March). A delicate balance. *Triathlete,* 90-92.

Mora, J.M. (1993, April 19). Tapering tips. *Running Times.*

Newby-Fraser, P. (1995). *Peak fitness for women.* Champaign, IL: Human Kinetics.

Plant, M. (1987). *Iron will.* Chicago: Contemporary Books.

Sheehan, G. (1989). *Personal best.* Emmaus, PA: Rodale.

Sherman, W.M. (1991). Carbohydrate feedings 1 h before exercise improves cycling performances. *American Journal of Clinical Nutrition,* 54:866-870.

Sherman, W.M. (1989). Pre-event nutrition. *Sports Science Exchange,* 1:12.

Sherman, W.M. (1989). Effects of 4 h preexercise carbohydrate feedings on cycling performance. *Medicine & Science in Sports & Exercise,* 21:598.

Sleamaker, R. (1997). *Endurance training for serious athletes.* Champaign, IL: Leisure Press.

Sullivan, M.E. (1993, January). Stretch—It feels good. *Current Health,* 4-5.

Taddei, S. (2000). Physical activity prevents age-related impairment in nitric oxide availability in elderly athletes. *Circulation, the Journal of the American Heart Association,* 101:2896-2901.

Thacker S. (2004). The impact of stretching on sports injury risk. *Medicine & Science in Sports & Exercise,* 36(3):371-378.

Work, J.A. (1991, January). Are java junkies poor sports? *Physician and Sportsmedicine,* 19:83-88.

Zawadzki, K.M., Yaspelskis, B.B. III, and Ivy, J.L. 1992. Carbohydrate-protein complex increases the rate of muscle glycogen storage after exercise. *Journal of Applied Physiology,* 72:1854.

Index